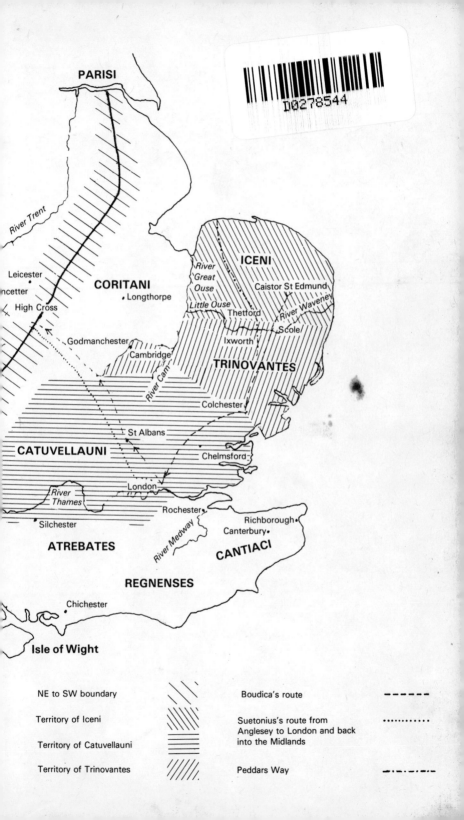

REBELLION AGAINST ROME

Boudica's uprising against the Roman
occupation forces in A.D.61

by

PLANTAGENET SOMERSET FRY

TERENCE DALTON LIMITED
LAVENHAM   .   SUFFOLK

1982

Published by
TERENCE DALTON LIMITED

ISBN 0 86138 014 2

Text photoset in 11/12 pt. Baskerville

Printed in Great Britain at
The Lavenham Press Limited, Lavenham, Suffolk
© Plantagenet Somerset Fry 1982

Contents

Index of Illustrations

Illustrations have been reproduced by kind permission of the following: Norfolk Museums Service — plates I, III, IV, & V; National Monuments Record — plate II; National Museum of Wales — plate VII; Suffolk Archaeological Unit — plate VIII; Norfolk Archaeological Unit — plate IX; Colchester and Essex Museum — plate X; Colchester Archaeological Trust — plate XI; and Cambridge University Collection — plate XII. Plates VI & XIII are by the author.

Preface

THIS is the story of Boudica and of the times in which she lived and led her celebrated revolt against the Roman occupation forces in Britain. It is a reconstruction, because we know nothing about her life except for the last few weeks of it, and even that dramatic period was described not by her or her people but by her enemies, the Romans. We can thus get but a glimpse of her life: the remainder has to be supplied by the imagination.

Boudica was probably the only woman ever to lead a revolt of major importance. For centuries she has been a folk-heroine of British history, and this must be because she was a champion of freedom, a battler for the underdog, a righter of wrongs, qualities British people seek in their leaders, and indeed in themselves. It must be more than coincidence that her statue was erected on a pedestal opposite the structure that houses the Mother of Parliaments.

Building up a picture of our first national heroine has been an absorbing task, and it is not without relevance that the work has been done in Norfolk and Suffolk, precisely the area in which she organized her revolt (though it spread into central England), the area in which I have my home. The work would not have been possible without very considerable kindness and assistance from Norfolk Archaeological Unit, in particular Tony Gregory, to whom I am very grateful. I do not see how anyone could write about Boudica without the aid of this Unit's remarkable sources of research and information on her territory and her times.

There is a considerable literature on late Celtic and early Romano-British history, and I have listed some of the works consulted. I am grateful to all these and many more for the inspiration they provided to dig into this most interesting period of our island story. I must also extend my deep gratitude to the President, David Williams, and the Fellows of Wolfson College, Cambridge, in continuing to make me welcome as a visiting scholar which has provided me with unparalleled facilities for research in Cambridge and ensured the most felicitous environment in which to write.

Finally, I want to thank Ann Meldrum for coping so efficiently with typing a very untidy manuscript, and as always my wife for many constructive suggestions she made for improving the text.

Plantagenet Somerset Fry
April 1982

Wattisfield, Suffolk,
& Cambridge.

CHAPTER ONE

Setting the Scene

IT WAS a spring morning in 61 A.D. Down at the water's
edge near Bangor on the Menai Strait between North Wales
and Anglesey, a grey-haired Roman general paced swiftly to
and fro along the sands between his tent and the prow of one of
a row of transport ships which were resting at anchor. As he
walked he rubbed his hands together vigorously, for there was
a nip in the air, as the sun was only beginning to rise. High in
the Snowdon mountains, snow was still packed around the
peaks as it always was at this time of year, and the winds sent
chill air down to the beaches. He noticed with interest the
sharp differences in the landscapes. On the mainland, it was
dark and mountainous; on the other side of the strait the
island was flat and the fields looked fresh and yellow from the
light of the rising sun. He could discern the movement of
warriors on the island shore, and he was glad that the next
battle would be fought on level ground.

The general was Gaius Suetonius Paullinus, Governor and
Commander-in-Chief of the Roman armies in Britain and one
of a group of first-rate commanders who had made their
names in tough but successful campaigns against Rome's
enemies. Now over 60, Suetonius could look back on a career
that included the consulship, the highest office of state under
the emperors, in 43. And on this chill morning he could feel
justly pleased with the results of his last two years campaigning
in central and northern Wales, following his swift march
through Cheshire and into the first of the Welsh hills. Britain
had seemed easy to overcome and perhaps would not be so
hard to govern.

Suetonius looked across the straits to Anglesey again. The
small, square island was so rich in cornfields that there was
enough to feed not only the population of Celts who, refusing
to accept Roman rule in the Welsh mainland, had sought
refuge in the island, but also to supply most of the communities remaining in the northern half of North Wales.

1

Stocked in barns and pits, the corn made Anglesey a granary for Wales and in future years it was to be called that. In the island, the druids, Celtic priests who were the spiritual leaders of British resistance to Rome and who had now taken over the military direction of resistance as well, stood at bay, marshalling the Britons into some kind of regimental order ready to fight to the last man. As the sun continued to rise, more flat-bottomed Roman transport ships were brought along the strait. They had been ordered from shipyards hastily set out in the estuary of the river Dee near Chester. And the men of Suetonius's legions, camped along the shore beside Bangor, rose from their tents, buckled on their cuirasses, and packed up their kit. At about nine o'clock the trumpeters sounded the call to get into the ships for the short journey across the water to Anglesey, and the men embarked quietly, without fuss, each one drilled to know exactly which place to occupy in his ship. Those who were rowing bent forwards and gripped their portions of the long oars with which the ships were propelled. The oarsmaster lifted his mallet and brought it down on to the anvil to begin beating out the rhythm for the oarsmen to follow. Thus, the armada set forth.

On the Anglesey shore stood the British army, with its dense throng of warriors. Between the ranks dashed women in black clothes, their hair dishevelled, waving torch fire brands and uttering horrible shrieks, giving encouragement in their own peculiar way. All round stood druids, lifting up their hands to Heaven, pouring forth dreadful curses.*

As the transports ground their forefoots into the Anglesey shingle, the legionaries leaped ashore — and for an instant stood still in their tracks, electrified as it were by the shrieking of the women, leaving them easy targets for British darts and sling stones. But it was a momentary hesitation and, urged by their centurions not to be put off by a lot of hysterical old crones, they carried their standards onwards, cut down all resistance, and set fire to the Britons' tents, using the British torches. Left and right they hacked and jabbed with their short, sharp swords. They ran on towards the sacred groves of the druids where tables had been laid out ready for victims for sacrifice — one of the more horrible customs of the druids which prompted the Romans never to spare them their lives if they were captured. They threw down the altars and slew the priests.

*Tacitus, *Annals,* xiv, 30 trans. Michael Grant, Penguin Classics, 1956, p. 317. All subsequent references to *The Annals* relate to this translation.

The victory was swift, complete and decisive, and it was achieved at very small cost in Roman lives.

But in the very moment of victory the Roman commander was brought some terrible news. A messenger, exhausted by hard riding from the relay staging post further back towards Chester, rushed into Suetonius's tent and collapsed, gasping at the commander's feet, clutching a tablet. The commander took it from the man's fingers and began reading. It contained news that the Iceni people in East Anglia had risen in revolt under the leadership of their queen, Boudica. She was aiming to drive the Romans right out of Britain. Slowly, Suetonius read the document. It was a detailed report from a legionary officer who had escaped from a fort somewhere, probably along a new Roman road in Suffolk, and it told of the happenings in East Anglia in the past few days. And as he read, Suetonius's expression changed from one of surprise to one of horror and alarm. One hundred thousand Britons, armed and very angry, led by their fiery queen, had besieged the Roman town of Colchester.* They had burned down its stone and wooden buildings, slaughtered everyone, whether Roman or British working for Romans.† No prisoners had been taken. ". . . they could not wait to cut throats, hang, burn and crucify." And, flushed with their grisly success, the host had started to move on down the road to Chelmsford, heading for London or St. Albans. The message did not say which.

There was one crumb of comfort in the dismal report. News had got through to Quintus Petillius Cerealis, the commander of Legio IX at Longthorpe, near Peterborough, and he was setting out at once with two vexillations‡ towards Essex to intercept the great rebel army. But the messenger was not to know that this force had already been severely defeated somewhere in Huntingdonshire by a detachment sent out by Boudica, and that Cerealis had barely escaped with his life.

The commander-in-chief dropped the tablet on the chair and let his arm fall. Just for an instant he could picture the situation at its very worst. Soon the whole population of Britain would join this terrifyingly successful woman com-

---

*Colchester was a *colonia*, a town inhabited by Roman or Latin citizens, who might be retired army veterans.

†A wattle and daub building solidified by the fire was excavated in 1965. See plate XI.

‡A vexillation was a detachment of a legion, of about 1,000 men.

mander, who had destroyed a Roman town and dared to aim at others. All his work — and that of his predecessors right back to old Aulus Plautius who had established the first bridgehead in southern Britain eighteen years earlier — would be swept away. Britain would be a Roman province no more. Then, Suetonius became the practical man again. He would take his cavalry at once down Watling Street, some 250 or so miles, to London, order the infantry to follow, and show this daring queen what a real Roman army could do. He barked out to his aide-de-camp to assemble all company commanders in his tent immediately. The man left, and Suetonius was alone for a moment.

What kind of woman was this Boudica, he wondered. He'd heard of her, of course, as the wife of Prasutagus, king of the Iceni. And as he reflected, the first of the company commanders appeared at the flap of the tent. Soon they were talking about the news. One of them had come across Boudica a few times and was telling Suetonius something about her standing with her people. Tactfully he was also trying to suggest what could have gone wrong in East Anglia.

*   *   *

What did Boudica look like? Was she anything like the famous statue of her, with her two daughters, on the Embankment at Westminster Bridge in London? The British of her time had no scribes to write things down. They have left no record of her appearance, no coins and no busts. The Roman historian Publius Cornelius Tacitus, who was married to the daughter of Julius Agricola, Governor of Britain from 77-84, wrote about the revolt. Born about five years before it, Tacitus must have met many people who had seen her, but disappointingly he did not describe her. Perhaps he thought his readers would already have seen likenesses done in stone by Italian sculptors, or drawings based on descriptions.

The only picture of Boudica that has survived is a description by the historian Dio Cassius (c. 150-c.235 A.D.), but it is vivid. She was of enormous build, terrifying to look at, with a harsh voice. A great mass of bright red hair fell to her knees. She wore a large twisted golden necklace and a multi-coloured tunic, over which was a thick cloak fastened by a brooch. Dio was portraying her haranguing her army before battle, and he added that as she grasped her spear she struck terror into the hearts of all who watched and listened.* And well she might! His unfinished portrait whets the appetite and stirs the imagination in us to supply the rest. Handsome rather than beautiful, with full mouth, deep, hypnotic eyes, firm jaw, broad shoulders and large breasts, Boudica sounds like the typical mother-figure that men of all ages have at some time or another wanted to dominate them. Such a woman would make a natural leader of a people whose freedom to live and work as they pleased had suddenly been threatened, whose possessions had been taken from them and on whom crippling new taxes had been imposed. For that is what happened to the Iceni people who lived in what are now Norfolk and parts of Suffolk, whose queen she was. Of all the tribes in the southern half of Britain the Iceni had given their Roman overlords the least trouble. Their king, Prasutagus, a man of great riches, had come to a happy arrangement with Rome whereby he remained a client-king in control of his kingdom. He may have agreed on a reasonable level of taxation in return, and it had been working well. But when he died, the Romans broke their part of the bargain, and they did so with great violence, cruelty and extortion. Their treachery and cruelty spared none, not even his widow, Boudica, or their daughters.

Prasutagus and Boudica had daughters but do not appear to have had sons. British tribes quite often chose royal women to succeed their kings. Indeed, the chief of the Brigantes, in northern Britain, was Cartimandua, who was ruling as queen at the time Prasutagus died. Boudica immediately assumed the leadership of her people—she may have been elected at a special gathering—and before long had whipped up very considerable support among neighbouring tribes like the Trinovantes to form a great confederation with one aim—to drive the hated Roman invaders and settlers out of Britain altogether. It was to be a war of independence and to be fought to the end.

The revolt was the climax of Boudica's life story. But it is the only part of her life about which there are any details. For reasons that will become clear later, it is likely that Boudica was in her forties when her husband died in 59. Before that, her history is a complete blank. According to the Roman historians, she was a member of a royal family in Britain, but

*Dio Cassius, *Epitome of Roman History*, Book lxii. 2., translated by E. Cary, Loeb Classical Library, 1968 impression, p. 85. All subsequent references to Dio's Roman History relate to this translation. NB. Dio calls Boudica 'Buduica' (in Greek, Βουδοῦικα).

not specifically of the Iceni. This enables us to reconstruct something of the kind of life she would have had from what we know about the history of the Celtic peoples, through the writings of Roman authors, from Celtic legends handed down verbally, and eventually put to paper in later centuries, and from archaeological finds. But it can only be a reconstruction.

We are on firmer ground with the revolt itself and how Suetonius dealt with it, for it was outlined by Tacitus twice, in two different books, and also by Dio Cassius.* How the Roman army operated, whether on the path of conquest or in emergency situations or even when simply policing the territories it had overrun, is well documented. And this documentation reveals, perhaps above everything else, the consistency with which the military machine functioned throughout the empire and when it was in conflict with the empire's neighbours. Commanders and their men followed much the same procedures whether they were fighting or controlling conquered peoples in the Atlas mountains of North Africa, on the banks of the Rhine in Germany or in the sands of Mesopotamia. It is not difficult, therefore, to trace the superior skill with which Suetonius outwitted Boudica and crushed her revolt once she had lost the initiative after the sack and destruction of St Albans.

Boudica's rebellion is one of the most famous events in Britain's story. For nineteen centuries, almost without interruption, it has been remembered in literature and legend as well as in history. The legend has filled in the gaps in her life story at the expense of the history. Some of the more imaginative eighteenth century antiquaries, for example, sought to establish where she was buried after her revolt collapsed and she took poison, and the mound in Parliament Hill Fields in London, and Harrow Weald, were two serious suggestions. A seventeenth century author even suggested that Boudica was buried at Stonehenge.† The sculptor Thomas Thornycroft, who made the statue on the Embankment at Westminster towards the end of the last century, fitted the axle bosses of her chariot with scythe blades. This led some historians writing of Romano-British times into thinking that that was a standard form of armament for the ancient Celtic

---

*Tacitus, *Annals*, xiv. 31-7, (pp. 317-21) and Tacitus, *Agricola*, xvi, trans. H. Mattingly, Penguin Classics 1964 impression, (pp. 66-67). All subsequent references to the *Agricola* relate to this translation. Dio Cassius, lxii, 1-12, (pp. 83-105).

†Edmund Bolton, *Nero Caesar, or Monarchie Depraved*, 1624.

chariot, until Sir Cyril Fox, in 1947, exploded the belief when he showed that the remains of Celtic chariots found in excavations at Llyn Cerrig Bach (in Anglesey) had no such fittings (see p. 13).

The appeal of the Boudica story is strong. Her military successes have been cited again and again to prove that women are at least as capable of leading men into battle as men, and she stands in a line of women commanders who have left an impressive record of gallant leadership in war, from the queen of the Amazons to Joan of Arc. But it should be said that Boudica's military successes were confined to attacks on undefended towns; when she came up against a prepared Roman army, she was routed. And yet, such things as we do know of her life amply justify her place in British history—and indeed in the long roll call of patriots of all ages—because she gave her life in the cause of liberty. If her story is presented free from the embellishment of legend, it is no less appealing for that.

CHAPTER TWO

The Celts in Europe and Britain

BOUDICA was Britain's first national heroine. She came from one of the tribes that made up the Celtic peoples in the British Isles. She lived nearly twenty centuries ago, during the time when Britain was invaded and much of it conquered by the Romans who, through a remarkable combination of military organization and political cunning, had built up an empire that occupied a substantial slice of the known world. It stretched from the north-west of Africa to the south-west of the Red Sea and from the Black Sea to Britain. And it was in Britain that Boudica challenged the might and authority of the Roman government, and came very near to driving the Roman forces of occupation out.

Boudica did not in the end succeed. What she did achieve, however, could not have been done by a leader of savage and uncultured barbarians, as her ancient British followers were once thought to have been. They were much more civilized than that. Indeed, they had been advancing for centuries, to such an extent that in her time many of their skills were as good as those of their conquerors, while their iron technology was probably better. To understand the background to the British revolt, we need to go back several centuries in time to look at the rise of Celtic civilization.

Boudica was Queen of the Iceni people, because she had been the wife of their king, Prasutagus, who died in 59 A.D. But we do not know if she was Icenian herself. Tacitus and Dio Cassius describe her as being of royal blood, but they do not say of which tribe.* Perhaps she was a high-born woman from one of the neighbouring tribes, the Trinovantes or the Coritani. But she was a Celt and very proud of it, proud of her ancient heritage, filled with the spirit of independence that is so characteristic of these interesting people.

What was their story? How did they come to be in Britain, after centuries as the dominant peoples in central Europe?

The change of a prehistoric people from barbarism to

*Tacitus, *Agricola*, xvi., (p. 66) and Dio Cassius, lxii, 2, (p. 85).

civilization comes when they begin to do more things for themselves than just hunt, kill and eat. Once they discover for themselves, or learn from others, how to plant corn and vegetable seeds, nurture the sown earth with water and then gather in the harvest, they become farmers as well as hunters. If they begin then to organize their lives, domesticate their animals, trade their farming products with their neighbours, build themselves homes of something more substantial than twigs and mud, and make tools, utensils and weapons of stone and metal, they come into the mainstream of history. And if they also develop a language, and perhaps even write it down in a script, and introduce the first steps in a number of native forms of art like sculpture and painting, then they have all the basic ingredients of civilization.

The ancestors of the Celts started out on this road to civilization in the vigorous air and unsettled skies of what is today Czechoslovakia, south Germany, Austria, Hungary and Switzerland, in about 5000 B.C., or perhaps even earlier. They farmed in this central part of Europe, whose land was for the most part of light soil called loess, a fertile earth which is built up by deposits carried along by the winds. They made use of the great rivers, the Danube and the Rhine, and their tributaries, to irrigate their fields and to move about from one place to another, probably on simply constructed rafts. They had a variety of utensils and tools made of stone, and they knew how to fabricate simple items of pottery from clay.

They were also able to construct substantial houses of timber. These were no mere huts of disorderly twigs and branches, covered with skins, such as prehistoric men put up for themselves in many parts of the world. They were well-built dwellings, such as the row of trapezoidal timber houses erected by fishermen on the Danube between 6,000 and 7,000 years ago, traces of which were recently found at Lepenski Vir in Yugoslavia. There have been other discoveries of dwelling remains of these times, from Czechoslovakia right across to Belgium. One long rectangular house, whose traces were found at Köln-Lindenthal on the Danube in Germany, seems to have been of advanced construction. Timber-framed, with thatched gabled roof, wooden lattice walls coated with clay, and doorways inside and out, this longhouse was probably a home for several families.

In time, these Europeans formed some kind of social

organization and developed skills and technologies, using the resources, particularly copper ores, that lay in the ground under their feet. At first, the copper was used for decorating objects. Then they discovered that by cold hammering, copper could be worked into utensils. The next step was annealing of copper by processes of heating and cooling and repeated hammering, to produce harder edges for tools and weapons. These Europeans also discovered smelting processes, and learned how to cast copper in moulds. Their metallurgical skills were given a boost by the discovery of bronze technology. Bronze is an alloy of copper and tin, and is much tougher than pure copper, and the resulting tools and weapons mark a new stage in the development of European civilization, the Bronze Age, which began in about 3000 B.C. There were considerable deposits of both copper and tin in Central Europe, and the availability of tin was particularly interesting to the concurrent civilizations of the Near East, which had never found plentiful supplies of it in their regions and were always looking for fresh sources. The Europeans thus had a desirable commodity and they began to learn something about long-distance trading.

At about this time, the Europeans began to form themselves into small kingdoms. These were farmed and in some cases marked out for cattle raising. A class structure arose in which the leaders, who possessed weapons of bronze, controlled, more or less according to the enthusiasm of the individual warriors concerned, all other inhabitants and activities within their boundaries. They separated themselves from humbler people by building larger and more sophisticated homes, by wearing distinctive ornamental jewellery round their necks and arms or clipped to their clothing, and by developing a ritual over the burial of their remains when they died. The continuing supply of raw copper and tin helped to keep them in power. But it seems that their weapons were employed much more for display and ceremonial than for fighting, which suggests they were not aggressive people. It is useful to remember this when considering their descendants, the Celts. Boudica, for example, did not go to war to build an empire but more simply to free her people from foreign domination.

All this was happening over a considerable period of time. The Bronze Age in Central Europe lasted for probably 2000 years from about 3000 B.C. to well into the first centuries after 1000 B.C. In the first years of the eleventh and tenth centuries

B.C. there emerged the Urnfield culture in Europe, whose peoples can be said to have been the first Celts. They are named after their custom of cremating their dead and burying the ashes in urns in graves which were levelled to the ground, and this differentiates them from those who came before, who raised huge mounds of earth over their dead (the Tumulus people).

The Urnfield people formed a language from a mixture of Indo-European tongues spoken in the Near East and southern Russia. It became the forerunner of the Celtic languages, six of which are still spoken today. The Urnfielders were more warlike than their predecessors. This may be because they wanted to protect their profitable metal mines. They developed new weapons, especially the heavy, slashing sword of bronze, which had decorated handle and hilt, and when, later, they learned the skill of iron-working, they became practically unconquerable. Some of their farmers began to use iron-tipped ploughshares, and this made them very rich, for better ploughing produced better harvests. By about the ninth century iron was being worked in most of the Urnfield areas, and in the areas of their descendants, the Hallstatt people. This marked the change in Central Europe from the Bronze to the Iron Age. The enthusiasm for making weapons should not, however obscure the very wide and fascinating variety of domestic and artistic articles the Europeans made from both bronze and iron, such as sculptures of animals, bowls, statu-ettes, bracelets and wine vessels.

The Hallstatt period covers about the years 700 to 500 B.C. in Central Europe. The name comes from the village of Hallstatt in Austria where, in the 1860s, archaeologists dis-covered an early Celtic Iron Age settlement of about the eighth century. Among the many finds was a cemetery with the graves of nearly 1,000 people. Another was a saltmine of the same date, and this is taken to suggest that the Hallstatt Celts traded salt with other civilizations, notably Greece and Etruria. Interestingly, the Hallstatt finds also showed that the people buried their dead in timber burial chambers over which they heaped mounds of earth. The Hallstatt Celts intermarried with more wanderers from the East, including people from Scythia, who knew how to breed horses and could manoeuvre them with very great skill. They brought horses into their new-found places of settlement, and thus introduced the horse

11

to central Europe. Remains of bronze and iron items of harness have been found in several sites. Horse breeding was to become a speciality of some later Celtic tribes, in particular, the Iceni in East Anglia. Horses figure widely on the coins of the Celts of the second and first centuries B.C. and the first century A.D.*

The Hallstatt settlement was not the only community of its kind, and other burial areas with similar finds have been discovered. We are really talking about a whole scattering of settlements in Europe when we use the phrase Hallstatters. There was another interesting feature. They evolved wagons with four wheels, each wheel with spokes, and clear traces of these have been found in burial chambers, where the wagons were generally used as biers for their owners. The Hallstatters were iron-using people, though bronze implements have been found. Most of their weapons were iron. They made axes for cutting down trees and scythes for harvesting corn and for removing high-growing grass. But the fabricators of these valuable weapons and tools were blacksmiths, specialists in ironworking who were not generally willing to share the secrets of their skills with ordinary people. They travelled about the countryside offering their services to warriors and farmers, and by keeping their secrets rose to high positions in European society.

How long the Hallstatters flourished we do not really know, but sometime in the sixth century their period gave way to another called the La Tène. This comes from the village of La Tène on the bank of the river Thièle that leads into Lake Neuchâtel in Switzerland. Here, in the middle of the nineteenth century, another exciting find was made by archaeologists. They discovered an accumulation of objects, many of them in metal, and these were linked with Hallstatt objects. But they were also distinctively in a fresh style, which we call the La Tène style. The objects dated from about 500 B.C., which is the end of the Hallstatt period. The centre of Celtic civilization had clearly moved westwards, developing along the way. One La Tène object found was a smaller, lightweight vehicle, a two-wheeled war-chariot, which was drawn by two horses yoked to a central pole. The wheels were spoked and wooden rims were fitted with an iron band round the perimeter, like a tyre. The chariot body was little more than a platform with two semi-circular sides, but with no front or rear framework.

*The development of horse designs on gold coins in Iron Age Britain is brilliantly summarized by A. K. Gregory in a Norfolk Museums Service Information pamphlet, *Iron Age Coinage in Norfolk*, 1977.

These war-chariots were a key weapon in Celtic warfare and were to loom large in the first conflicts between the Celts and the Romans in Britain.

During the Second World War Sir Cyril Fox examined a number of metal objects of the La Tène period found on the site of an aerodrome being built at Llyn Cerrig Bach, in Anglesey, North Wales. They included parts of wheels, hubs and other vehicle fittings, and he was able to suggest a reconstruction of a Celtic lightweight two-wheeled chariot.* A model was built and is now in the National Museum of Wales (Plate VII). It is similar to the La Tène chariots in use in Europe, relics of which have been found in graves along the Rhine and the Marne, and doubtless is the kind of chariot Julius Caesar wrote about in his description of British chariot warfare.

"The tactics employed by these charioteers are as follows. First they drive in every direction, hurling their javelins. Very often the sheer terror inspired by the galloping horses and the noise of the wheels throws their opponents into a state of confusion. Then they make their way through the squadrons of their own cavalry, leap down from the chariots, and fight on foot. Meanwhile the drivers retire a little from the battle and halt the chariots in a suitable position so that, if those who are now fighting on foot are hard pressed by the enemy, they will have an easy means of retreating to their own lines. So in their battles they combine the mobility of cavalry with the stamina of infantry. Daily training and practice have brought them to a remarkable state of efficiency. They are able, for example, to control their horses at full gallop on the steepest slopes, to pull them up and turn them in a moment, to run along the pole, stand on the yoke, and dart back again into the chariot."†

With the La Tène chariot at Neuchâtel was found a quantity of iron weapons, including an iron version of the slashing sword. The Celts would appear to have become more warlike. At about this time they began calling themselves Celts —in whatever way they spelled the name then. The Greeks referred to them as Keltoi and the Romans described them as

*Antiquaries Journal, xxvii (1947), p. 117.

†Caesar, Gallic War, Book IV, 33, trans. Rex Warner, Mentor Books, 1960, p. 85. All references to Caesar's account of his war in Gaul relate to this translation.

Celtici or Celtae, or in the case of the Celts who occupied what is now France, Galli. When Caesar talks about the Gauls, in his work on the Gallic Wars, he is referring to Celtic tribes with whom he clashed and whom he eventually overcame. They were speaking a tongue, with regional varieties, which was similar to modern Irish Gaelic, and they would probably have been understood perfectly well by specialists of the Celtic languages of this century.

Two exciting discoveries of Celtic tombs of the sixth and fourth centuries B.C. are central to our story. They were tombs of two women of very high rank, perhaps princesses or even ruling queens. One was at Vix, near Châtillon-sur-Seine, not far from Dijon in France. This was the grave of a young woman, about thirty years old, whose body was lying on the wooden floor of a four-wheeled wagon. The wheels had been taken off and were leaning against a wall of the chamber. Around the body were numerous finely-made objects, ornaments and utensils, including a golden crown and some bracelets. In the tomb were other interesting artefacts, such as a very large wine flagon of bronze, over five feet tall, which had clearly been made by a Greek craftsman. The Celts had been trading as far afield as Greece.

The other tomb was at Reinheim, near Saarbrucken, in Germany. Here, the woman had been buried in a richly furnished grave. The chamber was made of oak: inside were many gold objects, like an owl-headed torc (a necklace of twisted metal), bracelets, finger rings, and a bronze wine-flagon with spout.

The tombs of two women buried as if they had been chiefs do not, on their own, prove that women had equal rank with men in Celtic society, but they suggest that when the demand arose, the Celts would not hesitate to raise women to high rank, possibly to a position as head of a tribe or community. And this is borne out in the Celtic legends handed down generation after generation.

It is essential to remember this when considering the leadership of Boudica. The Sicilian-born historian, Diodorus Siculus (c.80-c.29 B.C.), commented that Celtic women were the equal of their husbands in stature and rivalled them in strength. No doubt they rivalled them in courage, too.*

*Ammianus Marcellinus (c.325-395 AD), in his *History of the Roman Empire*, xv. 12, 1-2, describes the effectiveness of one Gaul, assisted by his wife, against a whole troop of foreigners. They would not be able to withstand the pair, especially the wife when she swells her neck, gnashes her teeth and brandishes her sallow arms and strikes blows mingled with kicks . . .

In the fifth and fourth centuries B.C. the Celts spread in many directions. Some crossed the Pyrenees into Spain, where they mixed with native communities. They became the Celtiberians of Roman history. Some went eastwards into Asia Minor, where they fought the Greeks before settling down to form their own state, Galatia, At the beginning of the fourth century, hordes of Celts crossed the Alps into northern Italy, ravaged Etruria and, in 390, under their great chief, Brennus, sacked Rome. But this Celtic expansion did not last, and as the power of Rome, with its greatly superior organization, grew in Italy and extended beyond it, so the territories of the Celts in Europe shrank. By about 100 B.C. only Gaul, parts of Spain and the British Isles remained Celtic and independent. Half a century later, Gaul had been overcome in a nine-year war by the greatest soldier-statesman of all history, Julius Caesar, who made it a Roman province.

Almost the last stronghold of Celtic independence was Britain. Wanderer Celts had been coming across the Channel for centuries, ever since Hallstatt times. They came not as huge invading armies but in small groups, even individual family units. When they arrived, the island was already populated by remote relations, descendants of earlier Europeans who had drifted towards the more mountainous north and west parts, where the land is filled with hard rock formation, some of it volcanic. These regions are separated from the southern and eastern regions by a geological line called the Jurassic Ridge, a belt of well-drained limestone hills stretching roughly from Plymouth to Bristol and up to northeast Yorkshire. The land above the ridge was almost impossible to farm, though there was pasture for animals to graze. But below the ridge it was in many places very fertile. It was also well supplied with rivers and tributaries, which were of great value to settlers.

The movements of the Celts into Britain in the last centuries B.C. are not at all easy to chart. Recent excavations — and many have been initiated — have uncovered deposits of objects with such differences in style, age and origin that the pattern of settlements can only be outlined in general terms. The pattern may be divided into three kinds of Iron Age, A, B and C, but having said that, it is by no means so straightforward. The A, B and C ages are not strict measures of time. In general, Period A comes before Period B, but in some districts it lasts much longer than in others. B may start where A has not finished. C may not start at all. The settlements, however, help give us an idea of what kind of people Boudica led against the Romans, and what kind of background she herself had, for she was an Iron Age queen.

Iron Age Hallstatt Celts, grouped as Iron Age A people, colonized south-eastern England and East Anglia from about the eighth to the fifth centuries. Some were immigrants from Europe, some were traders who perhaps decided after several visits that they would like to live in Britain. Some became skilled farmers. They built settlements and fortified them. They were iron users and skilled potters, and many of their artefacts have been discovered. They settled in many areas. One settlement was at Fengate, near Peterborough, on the edge of East Anglia, previously a Bronze Age settlement. Another was at West Harling, in Norfolk.

The early Iron Age Celts spread across England and into Wales, and in some areas mingled with earlier Bronze Age people. Throughout the late Bronze Age and Iron Age they fortified their farms and community settlements with ditching, behind which were walls of timber posts or planks forming palisades, erected in raised earth banking. The Celts also began to build special forts on the tops of well-chosen hills, which had commanding views across the countryside. This kind of defensive work had already been erected in numerous areas of Europe, where it was sometimes reinforced with timber bracing bars. A fine example of an early Celtic hill fort in Britain is Cissbury in Sussex, probably erected in about 300, near the site of an earlier neolithic settlement that contained flint mines. About 60,000 tons of chalk had to be shifted to make the fort, and about 10,000 wooden posts about 15 feet tall were cut to reinforce the earth rampart.

Engineering works of this size suggest that the British Celts were in some danger. From the fifth to the third centuries B.C. a fresh series of invasions was launched by Iron Age intruders who are grouped in Britain as Iron Age B people. They came from France, chiefly from the basin of the river Marne. Mostly, they settled in Yorkshire. They also tried to colonize the south but were driven off. Some migrated as far as Cornwall and a few drifted from there upwards to the Midlands. The Yorkshire Marnians came to be known as the Parisi. They buried their dead along with their chariots in tombs. They produced very fine decorative metalwork. They also created a warrior class which took control of the inhabitants they found there, and pressed them into work.

In East Anglia, the Iron Age people appear to have done the same. Racing about the flat countryside in their two-wheeled chariots, they acted as a "trigger-happy" ruling class, or aristocracy, of warriors. They lorded it over the more peaceable Celtic inhabitants who had settled there generations earlier and founded villages, farmed the rich land, put livestock to pasture on the uplands, cleared huge areas of forest with their iron-bladed axes and converted it to fields, and set up small industries of pottery and weaving. The new masters were La Tène culture Celts, and they have left many examples of their decorative and ornamental skills behind. They also left many signs of their power, such as a sword of iron in a finely decorated bronze scabbard (found near Wisbech in Cambridgeshire), a dagger in a bronze sheath (near Bury St. Edmunds in Suffolk), part of a pony's harness (Newnham in Cambridgeshire), and an iron sword with decorated pommel depicting a sad human face (Shouldham in West Norfolk). But if they imposed their will upon the earlier inhabitants of East Anglia, they seem also to have mixed with them, in time producing a people of fiercely independent spirit whose urge to remain free was greatly helped by the geographical structure of the land in which they dwelt.

East Anglia, which consists of Norfolk, Suffolk and parts of the Fens of Cambridgeshire, and which juts out into the North Sea, is a district clearly separated from the rest of England by distinct geological and geographical features. The north and east sides are surrounded by the sea. The west side is bordered by a narrow strip of chalk-based land stretching from the north-west near Hunstanton and Snettisham down to the Downham-Ely district. To the west of that was soggy uninhabitable Fenland. Three sides of the rectangle were thus protected by natural features. Only the south had a more accessible border, much of which ran in a line roughly horizontal from east to west, from somewhere between Yarmouth and Ipswich on the East coast to an area lying in the Cambridge-Mildenhall-Brandon line.

This area of East Anglia became a separate "kingdom" of Celts, as it were, quite early on, and it was to remain so into Roman times. The gradual blending of the Iron Age A and

Iron Age B people evolved into a tribe, or perhaps a group of related tribes, which the Romans called the Iceni. South of this kingdom were another people, who occupied part of Suffolk and Essex, and were known to the Romans as the Trinovantes. It seems that for some time the two peoples managed to live side by side peacefully. Then, in about 100 B.C., southern Britain was again invaded, and the East Anglians felt threatened. Celts from France, Belgium and western Germany, known collectively to the Romans as the Belgae, came and settled, after a good deal of hard fighting with the inhabitants, in parts of Kent, Sussex, Hampshire and Dorset, and across the Thames in Hertfordshire and part of Essex.

The Belgae introduced the Iron Age C into Britain. They moved more swiftly than earlier invaders. It was, as one historian has put it* "a mass movement of warlike farmers and craftsmen who, sword in one hand, sickle in the other, established farms and *oppida*" (tribal capitals defended by ditch and rampart). They introduced improved farming techniques that enabled them to cultivate hitherto unfarmed (and unfarmable) stretches of land. They also seized hill-forts that belonged to Iron Age B people, notably the huge structure at Maiden Castle, in Dorset, where they enlarged the number of banks and ditches, strengthened the gateways and built up the arsenals of weapons and missiles. They also introduced the first coinage into Britain.

Between the years 59 and 50 B.C., Celtic Gaul was conquered by Julius Caesar (later to become master of the western world and founder of the Roman imperial system). During his campaigns he invaded Britain twice, in 55 and 54. The first invasion was a short-lived business and Caesar got little further than a few miles inland, where he frightened the British by his greatly superior military apparatus. He returned for a second attempt the next summer, defeated the British, by now under the leadership of a war-lord, Cassivelaunus, king of the Catuvellauni, a Belgic tribe in the Buckinghamshire-Hertfordshire-Bedfordshire area.

Caesar's first success was against the Britons of Kent. He marched towards the Thames, crossed it somewhere between Wandsworth and Westminster and headed into Hertfordshire. On the way he received an urgent appeal from agents of Mandubracius, a dispossessed Trinovantian prince whose capital was at Lexden (on the outskirts of Colchester) in Essex

*R. Rainbird Clarke, *East Anglia*, London. Thames & Hudson, 1960.

and who was now in exile in Gaul. They complained that the Trinovantes were being harassed by Cassivelaunus, who had his headquarters at Ravensburgh, some ten miles north-west of Wheathampstead in Hertfordshire. Caesar drew Cassivelaunus out of his hill-fort into battle and soundly defeated him, capturing the hill-fort. He gave the Belgic leader a stern warning to leave the Trinovantes alone, extracted sureties for the good behaviour of the Catuvellauni and set the arrangements down in a treaty. Then he returned to Gaul, after restoring Mandubracius to his position. The Catuvellauni shelved their ambitions in East Anglia — for the moment.

In his account of the two invasions of Britain, Caesar records that his quick and decisive response to the call of the Trinovantes for help prompted several other British tribes to send ambassadors to him to discuss terms for surrender.* It is clear that they strongly resented the aggressive activities of Cassivelaunus and his people and preferred to be on friendly terms with Rome.

One of the tribes listed by Caesar was the Cenimagni, who were probably the same people as the Iceni. It is not impossible, therefore, that one of their delegates was an ancestor of Prasutagus, king of the Iceni, Boudica's husband. With this first appearance of the Iceni in historical record, we are nearing the opening of Boudica's own life story.

About thirty years later, Cassivelaunus died. He appears to have kept to the treaty, but he was followed by his son (or grandson) Tasciovanus who soon broke the agreement and invaded Trinovantian territory, capturing their capital at Lexden (which the Trinovantes called Camulodunon). He began to issue coins there, bearing his name, but it seems that his sovereignty over the Trinovantes was short-lived, for before the end of the first century B.C., the latter had recovered their autonomy and their king, Addedomarus, was governing them from Camulodunon. It was his grave that was discovered in the excavations of the Lexden tumulus in 1924, which revealed an exciting haul of royal armour, jewellery, weapons, fragments of a golden-sheathed litter and so forth, which is now in the Colchester Museum. Addedomarus was defeated at a battle in or near Lexden by a chief from Kent, Dubnovellaunus, who was himself later driven out of East Anglia, in the first decade of the first century A.D., possibly 6 or 7.

Tasciovanus kept his tribal capital at Ravensburgh to begin

*Caesar, *Gallic War*, Book V, 20-22, (p. 97).

with, but towards the end of the first century B.C. he moved it to Verlamion (Prae Wood, near St Albans), a site above the valley of the Ver. He died in the first decade, but not before he had begun to share power with his son Cunobelinus (Shakespeare's Cymbeline). Cunobelinus re-opened the war against the Trinovantes — it was probably he who defeated Dubnovellaunus and drove him out of Essex, capturing Camulodunon, transferring the capital of his Catuvellaunian empire there, but not allowing Verlamion to run down. This was in 10 or 11 A.D., and it was a well-timed exercise, for it was immediately following the major defeat of the Roman army in Germany. Three legions under Quinctilius Varus had been cut to pieces by the German chief, Arminius, and this left Augustus short of enough forces with which to mount an invasion of Britain and deal with this breach of the Caesarian treaty.

Cunobelinus ruled for about 35 years. In that time he expanded his Catuvellaunian empire westwards into Berkshire, northwards through Bedfordshire to Northamptonshire, and north-eastwards into the territory adjoining — and perhaps in places actually belonging to — the Iceni. How far the forces of the great chief spread and settled can be judged to an extent by pottery finds, many of which display Belgic influences. They were made with the pottery wheel, a Belgic introduction into Britain. Coins also help to trace movements of British tribes in these times.

These leaders of the Iceni cannot have relished Cunobelinus's empire-building in the eastern Home Counties. They were seriously alarmed when forward detachments of Belgae moved into the Cambridgeshire-Suffolk depression between Newmarket and Thetford. Despite their natural defensive frontiers such as the river Ouse, the Fens and the woodlands of south Norfolk, the Iceni knew they could not rely entirely upon these to shield them from attack.

CHAPTER THREE

Boudica's Early Years

IT WOULD not be unreasonable to suggest that Boudica was born about 20 A.D. Her childhood and teens, even perhaps the first year or two of her marriage to Prasutagus, would all have taken place while Britain was still free from Roman dominion. Nothing is known about her early life, who her father and mother were, whether she received any formal education, and how she came to meet Prasutagus, because none of her contemporaries recorded anything about her. The Celts very seldom wrote anything down. They committed day-to-day events, descriptions of individual people and their achievements and so forth to memory, talked about them and relied upon their listeners to pass the words down from generation to generation. Sometimes their poets, or bards, sang the praises of a chief, or a famous band of warriors and its deeds, or perhaps an individual hero, in poetry or dramatic speech, and these survived in Celtic literature when, several centuries later, educated men began to write things down for posterity. One epic set down in the seventh century A.D. in Ireland was the Ulster Cycle of Stories, a collection of tales about the adventures of semi-legendary heroes, like Conchobar and CuChullain, who were larger than life (in much the same way as Hercules and Achilles of Greek legend), and who were chiefly concerned with fighting and cattle raiding.

If the deeds of the heroes were exaggerated, even fantastic, many of the descriptions of more ordinary things, such as what they ate, how they built their homes, what clothes they wore, are much more real, and it is from these that we can get an idea of how Boudica, as the daughter of a powerful and important Celtic chief, spent her young days. And we can tap the descriptions of Celts in the works of people like Pytheas, a Greek merchant from Massilia (Marseilles) who visited south-west Britain in the 320s B.C., Caesar, who had nine years in which to get to know the Celts in Gaul and Britain, and Diodorus Siculus, the Sicilian-born writer who flourished in the 30s B.C. and knew many Gauls. And there are the archaeological discoveries of the past century or two, painstakingly carried out by so many enthusiastic people.

Boudica lived as a young girl in the Celtic equivalent of a town, or *oppidum*. Celtic towns were like housing estates surrounded by stockades of timber posts, or ramparts and ditches, occasionally with both. In Britain some towns were small, with eight to a dozen houses inside a fortified enclosure (like Chysauster in Cornwall, which was not fortified), and some were several hundred acres in area inside strong fortifications, like Stanwick in Yorkshire. Some were on hill tops, like Maiden Castle in Dorset. The sites of many Celtic towns and villages have been found, and among them are Silchester in Berkshire (which became the site of a major Roman town later on), Glastonbury in Somerset (where the houses were mounted on an artificial island encircled by a lake and reached from the mainland by a causeway), or West Harling in Norfolk, which may have had only a few buildings in a simple enclosure, and dates from the seventh or sixth century B.C.

At Butser, near Horndean in Hampshire, round farmstead houses have been reconstructed in an interesting experiment, the Butser Ancient Farm Research Project, according to the ground plans of Iron Age Celtic houses discovered in excavations. The project is directed by Peter Reynolds. One house follows the plan of an Iron Age house found by Sir Mortimer Wheeler at Maiden Castle, in a major excavation (1934-7). At the Maiden Castle house, as it is called at Butser, the walls are of hazel wattle covered with daub (in this instance a mix of clay, earth, straw, animal hair (chiefly pigs'), grass, brambles, hay and other vegetable matter). The roof is a sharply pointed cone of thatch on ash rafters supported on posts, with hazel wattle under the thatch. There is no reason why this style of house might not have been built in East Anglia, too. Interestingly, there is no hole at the top of the roof for the smoke from the fire to escape; it is conjectured that smoke filtered through the thatch, killing insects as it went. It was also a good way to smoke joints of meat suspended from the rafters. Another reconstruction at Butser is the Balksbury House, of slightly different shape — and larger — with a porch.* A third reconstruction is the Pimperne house, large enough for the family of a Celt of high birth, perhaps even a branch of a royal family.

*The Butser farm is actually functioning as a going concern, with animals and crops such as would have been reared or grown during the Iron Age period. This "living laboratory" is open to the public.

Boudica's royal birth meant that she would have lived in a large house, big enough to have a dining room (or hall), several smaller rooms and some space for a servant or two. Some of the rooms might have been decorated with intricate carvings on the wooden posts and boards.

She would have come to accept the presence of weapons and armaments everywhere. The hall would have been festooned with weapons of all kinds, shields fixed to the walls, swords jabbed between cracks in the timberwork, daggers stuck in the thatching. The possession of weapons was of prime importance to all Celtic noblemen, warriors and people of free birth, and they were used as much for ceremonial and decoration as for fighting. When in 47 A.D. one of the early Roman governors, Ostorius Scapula, put a ban on the possession of weapons of all kinds throughout that part of Britain so far under Roman dominion or in alliance with Rome, it caused the greatest ill-feeling and resentment, and planted seeds of the revolt that blossomed with such ferocity in 61 A.D.

One of the features of Celtic society was the fostering of children in their very early years. Boys and girls were sent to live for several years with families of higher birth than themselves, receiving a comprehensive education. But royal Boudica would have stayed at home and been taught with children of other and lesser families.

There was greater equality between women and men in Celtic societies than in others. We have noted (p. 14) the comment of Diodorus Siculus that women were the equals of their men in courage and stature. Boudica was probably taught from an early age how to fight with both women and men, and she may have been trained by other women, for in some of the early Celtic stories there are tales of households where women taught young men and girls in the arts of warfare.

By her teens, Boudica was probably a skilled warrior. She may have had some battle experience, and we may be right in supposing she revealed qualities of leadership that were not to be forgotten and which were to be called upon in later years by her people. But Boudica also had the home life of a girl, and would have spent a lot of time decorating herself with ornaments, making herself up with the curious cosmetics that Celtic women used in those days. Girls let their hair grow very long and dressed it with care. They sometimes held it up with an assortment of interesting combs, remains of which have been found. They painted their finger-nails, dyed their eyebrows black with berry juice and used a kind of rouge called ruam on their cheeks. And to apply this make-up they used fine mirrors of bronze. One side was plain, smooth and highly polished, to produce a reflection that was perhaps a little distorted but good enough for what they wanted. The other side of the mirror was often most beautifully incised with scroll or foliage designs. One such mirror which has survived is the famous Desborough mirror from Northamptonshire, thought to have been made in the early first century A.D., which means that it could have been similar to one used by Boudica. There is another, the Birdlip mirror, from Gloucestershire. Both are in the La Tène style of decoration.

Before getting down to the make-up, most girls went to a great deal of trouble to get themselves clean. They bathed and washed often, using a kind of soap, and then scented their bodies with oils and herbs. After their toilette was over, they dressed. There was a choice of garments and a variety of fashions that would have pleased the twentieth century teenager. Celtic people, indeed, were well known for their distinctive and colourful clothing, and this was noted by many classical writers. They had introduced trousers into Europe; either they invented them or they adopted them from fashions of their ancestors from Scythia. Both sexes wore them, though they were more favoured by men. Trousers were garments of linen or wool, and often in gay colours and patterns, such as big black and yellow diamond shaped checks. Some trousers were knee-length and tight-fitting, some went more loosely down to the ankles. Though it is easy to visualize Boudica dressed when in command of her armies in a many-coloured tunic of linen down to her feet, covered with a woollen cloak, because she is thus described by Dio Cassius, it is possible that she also wore the latest in East Anglian jeans of the time. Her cloak was probably sleeveless, fastened round her neck with one of her many silver brooches, clipped by safety pin. But sometimes she wore a poncho type of cloak, in multi-coloured wools. Her tunic was belted at the waist with a girdle of wool rope, which may have had jewelled ends or was clasped by gold bands near the end knots. The most popular colours seem to have been green and red, which would have showed off her flowing auburn hair. One of her cloaks may have been striped or flecked, with gold braid round the edges, like those seen and described by Diodorus and by the Roman administrator Pliny the Younger.* The cloaks worn by the Celts often marked the position their wearers held in society. One Irish saga tells of king's cloaks having five folds. And the great number and variety of fine woollen cloaks worn among the Celts suggests a thriving sheep rearing industry and a widespread activity in weaving.

Celtic men and women wore a great deal of jewellery, brooches to hold cloaks around their necks, gold and silver ornaments with intricate animal designs on their tunics, at shoulder and at waist level, beads on the ends of plaits in their women's hair, gold thread woven into the silk of their tunics, rings on their fingers, simple and complicated, in solid carved gold or jewelled, bracelets of gold or bronze, torcs of gold for their heads or round their necks. And the obsession with jewellery spread to their weapons. Iron swords had bronze hilts, iron spearheads were decorated with bronze inlays, daggers had elaborately carved sheaths, bronze helmets were decorated with enamel, and shields with red glass studs embedded in the swirling designs on the front have been found. At any time after she was about fifteen, Boudica would have looked magnificent in her royal apparel.

There were no schools in Britain in her young days. Her education was probably limited to the use of arms, domestic skills and, perhaps, one or two crafts, such as pottery and embroidery. How to recite the deeds of her family, her ancestors and the Celtic tribes of Britain would have been learned from poets and orators who, perhaps, taught her how to use words to powerful effect. Both Tacitus and Dio Cassius draw attention to the stirring language she used to whip up energy and enthusiasm when she led her people into battle.†
And the lack of writing skills among the Celts encouraged in them a remarkable ability to memorize great quantities of speeches, anecdotes and legends, as well as much factual matter. Passed down seven or eight times, the wording would have altered relatively little. Compare that with today. If you tell a story to a friend, and he passes it on to another, and that person repeats it to a fourth, and so on, until a seventh relates what he has been told by the sixth, the result is so different from the original it is almost unrecognisable. Boudica was also

*Gaius Plinius Secundus (c.61-113 AD).

†Tacitus, *Annals*, xiv, 35, (p. 320), Dio Cassius, lxii, 3-5, (pp. 85ff).

brought up to accept certain religious teachings and to take part in some rituals, probably instructed by the Druids.

By the time she was twenty, about 40 A.D., Boudica was able to hold her own among men and women in her father's circle in East Anglia. She had met most of the visitors to her father's town, and she had probably travelled widely about southern Britain where she would have met Roman traders and adventurers. She would have learned much about the Roman Empire, how it worked and what it was like to live under Roman dominion in Gaul. She would also have met descendants of those who fought against Julius Caesar at the battle at Ravensburgh in 54 B.C. She may even have been introduced to Cunobelinus, whose great-grandfather Cassivellaunus was beaten by Caesar. And she would certainly have known all about Cunobelinus's attempts to spread his Catuvellaunian empire throughout southern Britain.

Cunobelinus was ageing now, after nearly thirty years as king, and at his palace at Camulodunon, his tribal capital, two of his sons, Caratacus and Togodumnus, were gradually taking over his government. They persuaded the old man to banish their brother Adminius to Gaul and were openly planning to invade other tribal regions, among them the land of the Iceni. Sometime in 41 or 42 they also drove Verica, king of the Belgic Atrebates tribe in Berkshire and Hampshire, into Gaul and moved into his kingdom.

The threat to the Iceni was very great. The natural frontiers of their territory were not such that a resolute attack by the Catuvellauni would necessarily fail, and the Iceni leaders realized they had to get together to build up their military strength to resist aggression successfully. This could be done, as it had before, by treaties or alliances between tribes, sealed by marriages between members of the royal families. Boudica was one very marriageable daughter of a chief in or near East Anglia, and it is possible that she was betrothed to Prasutagus at this time. Prasutagus may, in fact, have been a son or brother of the Icenian king, or he may have become king of the Iceni by then. But whether prince or king, the marriage was appropriate and it strengthened the position of the Iceni.

When Adminius was banished to Gaul, he appealed to the Roman Emperor Gaius (37-41 A.D.) to compel Cunobelinus to reinstate him. It had long been the Roman government's policy not to interfere in British matters. The emperor

Augustus had set the north-west boundary of the empire as the coast of Gaul, and his successor Tiberius had observed it. But the insane Gaius (Caligula) who followed decided to respond. He took an expeditionary force to the coast of Normandy with the aim of invading Britain, but as the men were actually assembling on the shores, he changed his mind, it is thought, because the men refused to cross the Channel.*

Later in 42, by which time Cunobelinus had died, the exiled Atrebatic king Verica decided to appeal to Caligula's successor, Claudius, for help in recovering his kingdom. Claudius considered responding to the appeal. There were several good reasons for taking up where Caesar had left off in 54 B.C. The government had been watching the land-grabbing activities of Cunobelinus and of his sons, Caratacus and Togodumnus, who were building up an unacceptable power base. The British leaders had had the nerve to demand from Rome the extradition of Verica and Adminius, and when this was refused, had begun to "create disturbances on the Gallic coast". There were strong economic incentives for attempting the conquest of Britain: the island was rich in metals like iron, lead, copper and there was some gold. There were commodities like wool and cattle, and of course natives for the Roman slave markets. And there was the long-held belief among all Romans that their civilization, their way of life, their practical genius were better than those of any other people in the world. They did not accept that there was any part of the world "where they had no legal or moral right to be". The poet Virgil, who cried that Jupiter had bestowed upon the Romans empire without limit† and the historian Livy who claimed that "no human power shall be able to resist the military might of Rome", ‡ were only giving voice to what every one of their countrymen felt to be a god-given destiny, to rule everywhere. More specifically, so far as Britain was concerned, the Romans detested the Druids and their influence, and considered their religious and sacrificial practices degrading. And as long as the Britons remained unconquered, they constituted a permanent danger to the stability of Gaul, for the Gauls and the Britons were kin. What the Romans did not calculate, how-

---

*This lunatic then ordered the troops to collect sea shells. Box loads were gathered up and transported to Rome where they were publicly displayed as booty won by Caligula in his successful campaign against Neptune, God of the Sea!

†*Aeneid*, i. 278ff.
‡*History*, I. xvi. 7.

ever, was that holding Britain down was going to involve them in maintaining up to 50,000 legionaries and auxiliaries in more or less permanent military readiness for about four centuries. This commitment represented keeping an army in Britain of about one tenth of the total military strength of the empire, a commitment hardly proportionate to the value of the province.

Claudius discussed the matter of Verica's appeal with his advisers who favoured an invasion, straightaway if possible, for some of the preparations for Caligula's adventure a year or two earlier will not yet have been dismantled. Aulus Plautius, governor of Pannonia (now part of Yugoslavia), who had been consul in 29, was chosen to command the forces.

Even in the first century A.D., news travelled quickly, and reports of the projected invasion reached the island long before the troops embarked on the coast of Gaul. The size of the invasion armada was probably not reported accurately, but whatever did get through will have startled the dominant Catuvellauni. Caratacus, who controlled Hampshire, Surrey and part of Kent, and Togodumnus who governed Essex, Hertfordshire and parts of Suffolk and Cambridgeshire, probably met to discuss the threat, as they heard it, and make plans to resist it down on the Kent coast. How confident they were of beating off an assault by the greatest military power in the world we do not know, but they may have been lulled into thinking that only a small force would be sent to demonstrate Roman displeasure at their activities, perhaps one on the same scale as that of Julius Caesar's, 98 years before. But it was to be a much greater affair.

The Iceni had also received the first reports of Roman intentions, and to them the news came as a great relief. The Catuvellauni would have to withdraw a substantial part of their forces from East Anglia to deal with the Roman landings, and this would lift the pressure off the Icenian frontiers. For the first time in a generation the people of the Iceni would be able to feel safe.

CHAPTER FOUR

The Invasion of Britain and the
Seeds of Revolt

THE decision of the Emperor Claudius to invade Britain was translated into action without delay. By the end of the year (42) the machinery for assembling and equipping a large army in north-west Gaul had been set in motion. Detailed consideration was given to the accounts of both Julius Caesar's invasions, notably the masterly summaries that he wrote at the time. Lessons were drawn from the difficulties he had met and the successes he had won. Claudius was determined that nothing should be left undone which might give him success.

The emperor and his advisers reckoned that four legions (about 5,500 men in each), together with auxiliaries and a special force of cavalry, amounting to about 40,000 men in all, should be enough. The legions picked were all battle-experienced. Legio IX *Hispana* was summoned from Pannonia where it had been at the disposal of Aulus Plautius, the Governor, who was commander-in-chief designate for the British expedition. He was about sixty and had years of sound, if unspectacular, experience behind him. He set out from his province with the legion, and arrived in north-west Gaul after a journey of more than a thousand miles. There he found three other legions, all from the Rhine district, waiting — Legio II *Augusta*, commanded by Titus Flavius Sabinus Vespasianus (who was to become Emperor Vespasian in 69), Legio XIV *Gemina* and Legio XX *Valeria*. The commanders were Vespasian's brother Sabinus, and Hosidius Geta.

There was a fifth, Legio VIII, and this was to be held in reserve. The special cavalry force was under the command of Didius Gallus, who was later (in 52) to become Governor of Britain. And the auxiliaries assembled there consisted of lightly armed non-Roman troops — archers, stone-slingers and javelin throwers from Gaul, Germany and Thrace. The

29

Romans were accustomed to employing foreign troops from nations they had conquered, or with whom they had treaties of alliance, but they kept them in military formations separate from their own legions.

By about March, 43, preparations for embarking the armada were complete. The specialist corps of engineers, blacksmiths, carpenters and so forth, who repaired armour, kept siege engines working, designed and laid out fortifications and camps, built bridges and towers, and shod horses, were also assembled, the first stages of their work done. The supply department had almost finished filling up the holds of the ships with quantities of stores, clothes, boots, extra weapons, spades, tools, food and jars of wine, and the other things invading armies of those days needed. Food supplies were kept small because Roman armies depended very largely upon what they could forage in the lands in which they were campaigning.

The centurions in the legions had checked that their men had all the required equipment — and what a lot each legionary had to carry! He was a foot-soldier, and he wore thick-soled sandals or hob-nailed shoes. He was dressed in iron or hardened leather armour under which he wore a sleeveless woollen tunic. He wore a bronze crested helmet, carried a semi-cylindrical shield of three layers of plane plywood, about ¼ inch thick, covered with parchment or calf-skin, with its edges rimmed with metal or leather, and having a central boss, and he was armed with a short sword which was effective for cutting as well as thrusting. He carried a *pilum*, a heavy throwing javelin, which was about seven feet long. This had a long thin iron which continued into the wooden shaft for some distance. The pilum was hurled at the enemy, and immediately it struck an opponent's shield it bent downwards, immobilising it very effectively.

While on the march, the legionary carried everything he needed on his back — armour, stakes for a trench, saw, basket, spade, axe, cooking pot and a supply of corn, as well as his weapons and shield. The weight came to more than fifty pounds. The heavier baggage, like tents and the component parts of mechanical weapons (such as a ballista), were carried on wagons or by baggage animals.

Dressed and loaded up, the legionary crossed the Channel, and had to be ready to jump off the ship the instant it ran aground and enter into the fray as he splashed on to the wet sand. In Caesar's time, vigorous assaults of this kind on the beach on the Kent coast startled the British and won the Romans a tactical advantage in the first few hours.

The troops were about to board their transports and the armada to set sail when, suddenly, there was a clatter of swords and shields. At one end of the troop line some men had begun to beat their swords against their shields, slowly and in time, and then more quickly. The banging was taken up by the next group of men and so on right down the line, until the whole army was beating out in unison. It was one of the standard ways in which Roman troops protested. This time, they were refusing to embark. They dreaded crossing the Channel. To them it was like stepping off the edge of the world and they were not going to do that, not even for the emperor.

It was a full scale mutiny. What would the commander-in-chief do? Would he respond like Julius Caesar who, once faced with a similar refusal by his men to move, ran out in front of them and addressed them as "Citizens". The insult to seasoned troops stung them into remorse, and in a flash they begged to be pardoned for flagging. But Aulus Plautius was no Caesar, and in addition, all but his own Pannonian legion were unknown to him. So, ordering a halt, he sent an urgent message by fast riders to the emperor. Claudius responded at once by sending one of his principal ministers, Narcissus, a former slave of great intelligence and cunning. Narcissus reached northern French coast a few weeks later and harangued the troops. At first they resented being addressed by an ex-slave, but he cracked a few jokes and got them into a better mood.

Late in April or early in May the great armada finally set sail, in three squadrons. It has been thought that the landing in Britain took place in three separate places, Lympne, Dover and Richborough, deliberately to fox the enemy and force him to divide his forces. But the evidence is now that the bulk of the force landed only at Richborough. The commander-in-chief was pleasantly surprised to find no British forces waiting to repel his troops. The British had withdrawn. The landings were accomplished without hindrance, and before the British could in any sense rally Aulus Plautius had his whole army ashore and a considerable stores base built up.

What had happened? Caratacus and Togodumnus, waiting in east Kent for the Roman invasion fleet to reach the coast in the Spring, had got news of the troops' refusal to embark. Probably they chuckled as they gave the orders for their forces to disperse and head back towards the London area. The Romans had lost their nerve! The mutiny thus turned out to be a blessing in disguise for the invaders, for the most difficult part of any invasion by sea is to make a firm landing and get the armies and their equipment off the ships and on to the shore, where a bridgehead has to be established immediately. It was Aulus Plautius's turn to chuckle.

No time was wasted, once the landings had been completed. The legions were provisioned and ordered to advance north-westwards towards the River Medway. This was the first major geographical obstacle on the way to the Home Counties, the centre of Catuvellaunian power. It was Plautius's aim to clear Kent of resistance and then head for north of the Thames. It was generally Roman policy when invading territories occupied by several tribes to try to break up alliances between them, and Plautius probably considered isolating Caratacus from his brother Togodumnus. A battle was fought on the Medway where the two British leaders were taken completely by surprise by the skill with which the Roman legionaries got themselves across the river in battle order and reached the other side instantly ready to attack. The British were routed, notably by a sharp assault by men under Vespasian, and fled towards London where they crossed the Thames. Plautius pursued them, and somewhere near Westminster he built a temporary bridge and took his army across, again taking the British by surprise. Once over the river, he learned that Togodumnus had been killed, probably in a skirmish with Roman forward patrols. This left the Essex and Hertfordshire part of the Catuvellauni lands leaderless. Caratacus, stunned by the news of his brother's death, hesitated whether to race for Essex and fight it out or flee westwards and whip up support among the tribes there, among them the Dobunni, the Durotriges and the Silures, who could, perhaps, join in an anti-Roman axis. He elected to go west, and Plautius chose not to pursue him, for the eastern kingdom was there for the taking. But he did not move eastwards, either. Instead, he sent messengers to Rome to tell the emperor that he had crossed the Thames, having defeated the first of the British armies sent against him. Would Claudius like to exercise his imperial privilege of leading the Roman forces into the capital city of the enemy? Whatever else may be said of the lame and stuttering ruler of the Roman world, whom some considered an idiot, Claudius had a strong sense of historical occasion. Author of several important histories, he had long wanted to take part in an actual military campaign but his disabilities had prevented it. Now the chance had come, and he seized it. The messengers were sent back to Plautius to announce that he was coming to Britain as soon as he could get there.

Plautius, meanwhile, consolidated his positions in south-east Britain, putting down resistance in various quarters. He also moved into one or two British towns and began the process of Romanising them, starting to mark out the first areas for military settlement. To these he would encourage some soldiers due for retirement, organize cash grants for them and hope also to attract some traders from Gaul to set up simple workshops and stores in swiftly erected timber buildings. British people in the countryside who had decided not to resist Roman rule would also have been encouraged to come into these areas and get a taste of what superior organization could offer. One of these was what came to be called Verulamium (St Alban's) in Hertfordshire, begun lower down the valley near Prae Wood, the Catuvellaunians' former capital. It is thought the people in this area chose to yield to Aulus Plautius as soon as his troops appeared in the district, and in return Verulamium was granted a charter as a *municipium* early on in the occupation.*

As well as embarking upon these administrative measures, Aulus Plautius turned his attention to the western part of Britain where Caratacus had fled. He ordered Vespasian to wrap up British resistance in the south and to head into Dorsetshire. This large, thick set, energetic man of action, with heavy jowl and broad nose, was to display great military skill and leadership, and in a swift campaign conquered the Isle of Wight, most of Hampshire and all Dorset, beating the British (probably the Durotriges) in a great battle at Maiden Castle, one of their largest and most heavily defended hill-forts.

*The date of the granting of *municipium* status to Verulamium (i.e., a town with Roman and/or Latin rights) is contested. Prof. S. S. Frere argues in *Britannia* (Routledge, Kegan Paul, 1978 edn., pp. 98-99), for the time of Claudius (41-54 AD), but John Wacher, in *The Towns of Roman Britain* (Batsford, 1978 impression, pp. 18-19), puts the case for the years of Vespasian's reign as emperor, 69-79. Tacitus wrote of Verulamium as a *municipium* at the time of the Boudica rebellion, but it is not clear if he was referring to it as such in that year or at the time in which he was writing, viz. early 2nd century AD.

In the last days of August (43), somewhere near Boulogne, on the north-west coast of Gaul, Claudius formally took over the command of some reserve forces and brought them across the Channel in an uneventful voyage to Richborough. Among the animals he had transported were a few elephants. He moved rapidly north-westwards from the Kent coast to the Thames, crossed it probably near Dartford and joined Aulus Plautius and his legions in south-west Essex. As he approached the vast encampment of his general, the emperor could smell the salt air blowing up from the estuary and see the glint of the standards and weapons of the troops as they raised the shout "Imperator" again and again across the flat fields.

No time was wasted. Claudius gave the order to advance eastwards and at once some 30,000 Romans tramped along the muddy road to Camulodunon. Within a week, after at least one short battle with Catuvellaunian guerillas, the emperor reached the royal capital of Cunobelinus. On the way in at Lexden, he passed the huge mound which was the grave of Addedomarus. The conquest of south-east Britain seemed complete, and the emperor marked it with a ceremony of triumph. He entered the capital in the imperial car, flanked by the elephants. There he received the surrender of the town's defenders, and it is recorded that eleven British kings also submitted to him, offering treaties. For "kings" one may read "chiefs" in most instances. Some of them had not been involved in the fighting, and were either frightened into submission or saw that it was politically wise to come to terms. Among the latter were Cogidubnus, ruler of Sussex,* and Prasutagus, one of the kings of the Iceni, who may well have been accompanied to Camulodunon by his wife, Boudica. A settlement was imposed by Claudius on the territories so far won, roughly those lying below the line from Colchester to Portsmouth. Agreements were made with some of the eleven kings, by which the new province of Britannia was to be governed by Rome or through the agency of these kings in subordination to the Empire.

Claudius did not linger in Britain. He stayed just long enough to agree the site for a new temple to be named after him, to celebrate his victory. It would be in the centre of a new Roman town, which we shall call Colchester from now on, to be built just beside the original Camulodunon, and in time the two would merge. Then he set out for Rome. His stay in

---

*Cogidubnus may have been the son of Verica, the Atrebatic king expelled by Cunobelinus's sons in 42, and was probably put in power as client-king in Sussex by Claudius.

Britain is said to have lasted but sixteen days, but more probably ran to several weeks. On his return to Rome he celebrated a triumph, the Senate gave him the title "Britannicus" to add to his already long list of names and titles, and decreed that two triumphal arches should be built to commemorate his deeds. Part of the inscription over one arch, in Rome, has survived, and it has been reconstructed with what is thought to be the missing wording. It reads, in translation:

> "To the Emperor Tiberius Claudius, son of Drusus, Caesar Augustus Germanicus, Pontifex Maximus, Tribunician power for the eleventh time, Consul for the fifth time, saluted as Imperator twenty-two times, Censor, Father of his Country. (Set up by) the Senate and People of Rome because he received the formal submission of eleven Kings of the Britons, overcome without any loss, and because he was the first to bring barbarian peoples across the Ocean under the sway of the Roman people."*

The settlement that Claudius arranged for Britain is central to our story. Before it, the British Celtic tribes, often at war with each other (and in the case of the Belgae, since the first century B.C., dominating their immediate neighbours), were all free from Roman rule and were determined to keep it that way. After it, many of the tribes threw in their lot with Rome and agreed to live within the framework of the imperial system, content to accept rules and restrictions unthinkable only a generation before. How this arrangement worked was to depend upon how the system was imposed, and upon the characters and actions of those sent by the Roman government to control the new province. The great tragedy of early Romano-British relations lies in the ill-judged and unfeeling policies that followed the settlement. Seeds of revolt were sewn in East Anglia almost as soon as Claudius left the country. One example was the granting of favoured status upon St Albans, a town peopled by some Catuvellaunians who had chosen to yield to Rome and not to join the resistance led by Caratacus and Togodumnus. It marked down the inhabitants as traitors to the British cause: one day they would have to pay for being collaborators.

Soon after Claudius had gone, Aulus Plautius proceeded with the next phase of his plan of conquest. The Claudian settlement had secured the neutrality of Prasutagus of the

*Translation from *The Roman Conquest of Britain*. Webster & Dudley, 1973 edition, p. 165.

Iceni, of Cogidubnus of Sussex and of Cartimandua, queen of the Brigantes, who ruled over an area covering approximately the northern Midlands and Lancashire and Yorkshire. This left the southern Midlands, the west country and Wales as the next districts to be pacified. And over in the west Caratacus, a notable absentee from the delegation of eleven kings at Colchester, was energetically forming a coalition of tribes to continue the struggle for British freedom. During the next four years the Roman forces gradually extended their occupation, so that by 47 all Britain below a line running from somewhere south of the Humber to Exeter, through Lincolnshire, the Midlands and the Cotswolds, was under Roman government or client-kings. The line was reinforced by maintaining a broad belt, about 25-30 miles wide, which was designated as a military area, from north east to south west along it. This broad band included a new road that came to be known as Fosse Way, many stretches of which remain visible and are used, albeit with new surfaces, today.

Aulus Plautius had good reason to believe that a large part of the province was safe and settled, and he could look forward to his retirement in Italy. But when his successor, Publius Ostorius Scapula, arrived in Britain in 47, he found the province, as Tacitus put it, in chaos. "Convinced that a new commander, with an unfamiliar army and with winter begun, would not fight them, hostile tribes had broken violently into the Roman province".* What had happened was that Caratacus, at the head of a combination of tribal armies, had taken advantage of the change-over and had attacked and broken through the military broad belt somewhere in the Cotswolds.

The new governor responded swiftly by chasing the Celtic forces out, pushing them back across the Severn and the Wye, whence they had come. This led him into difficult territory, the lands of the Deceangli of the north-east of Wales and the Silures of the south, and it opened up the prospect of a long-drawn-out campaign, largely of mountain warfare, where the inhabitants could more or less choose the ground on which they would fight. For some time the Celts in Wales backed Caratacus, appointing him their leader and providing him with men and weapons to keep up guerilla warfare. In 51, leading some 10,000 men, Caratacus risked a battle on open ground of his choosing, somewhere in mid-Wales, but he was

*Tacitus, *Annals*, xii. 31 (p.256).

out-manoeuvred and defeated through the superior discipline and equipment of the Roman troops. Two sites have been suggested: Cefncarnedd, near Caersws, and the hills near Dolforwyn.

Caratacus escaped, and fled to the kingdom of the Brigantes, whose queen, Cartimandua, had come to terms with Rome in 43. She was a client-queen. He tried to get her to carry on the struggle against Rome but he had misunderstood the extent of her dependence upon Rome. A client-king had limited independence; the self-governing powers he had were for his life-time only. He might be made a Roman citizen, but this did not necessarily compensate for the restrictions on his movements and administrative activities. He was not normally allowed to mint his own coinage, he could not make alliances or treaties with other nations without permission, and he could not refuse to let his fighting troops be employed by Rome in her armies if they were needed.

Cartimandua had Caratacus put in chains and she sent him under escort to Ostorius who sent him on, with his wife and children, to Rome. There, Claudius displayed them before the mob, who were agog to see the man who had for years defied the Roman army in that remote island off the coast of Gaul. When Caratacus was brought before the dais on which the emperor and his wife, Agrippina, sat in splendour on their golden thrones, he spoke out:

> "If my royal birth and my rank had been accompanied by moderate success in war, I should be here in this city today as your friend and not as your prisoner. As it is, I am humbled while your day is a day of glory. You are surprised that I regret having nothing left but my life and honour. But why should you be? If you want to be master of the world, does it follow that everyone else should want to be your slave? If you want your day of glory to be remembered, don't put me to death, as is your country's custom. That would soon be forgotten. Spare me instead, and history will remember your clemency for ever."

Claudius, always quick to rise to the occasion, warmed at once to the brave words of the defeated champion of Celtic freedom, ordered his chains and those of his family to be taken off, and offered him a home in Italy. Caratacus was glad to accept, but he could not help saying to the Emperor, as he looked around and marvelled at the great buildings of stone and marble, "With so many wonderful buildings here, why do you want our poor British huts?"*

The removal of Caratacus from the scene did not put an end to Rome's difficulties in Britain. Many of these were the fault of the governors and their administrations. When Caratacus first breached the military broad belt in 47, Ostorius reacted swiftly and drove him out. Then Ostorius did something else that was to cost Rome dear. He decided to disarm all the British people below the Fosse Way, people who were already part of the province and could be presumed loyal. This meant a systematic house-to-house search in every town, village and community, to see that the governor's decree that every British subject should surrender all arms was being carried out, and promptly. Now, to the Celts the bearing of arms was one of their most prized rights. Their great war leaders believed that their individual weapons were inhabited by gods, and every man who had a weapon looked upon it as a friend, a relation, a being with life in it, that would act in concert with him who held it. Great skill and loving care were often lavished on the decorating of weapons, as we have seen, and when weapons were not in use they were generally on display or put away into comfortable protection, out of harm's way. To take away a Celt's arms was like taking away his manhood, like Samson losing his great locks of hair. It was bad enough to disarm the British in those areas that had fought Rome and been defeated. It was far worse to extend the penalty to the peoples who had voluntarily allied themselves to Rome in peace, like the people of Cogidubnus's Sussex and, more particularly, the Iceni.

The Iceni, proud and independent, but since 43, nonetheless grateful to Rome for lifting the Catuvellaunian danger off their frontiers, felt the insult very deeply indeed. One can imagine the reaction of Prasutagus, and doubtless, the other chiefs of the Iceni, and of his wife, Boudica. Ostorius was treating them no better than he treated Caratacus, who had been organizing guerilla warfare for years. What was a treaty with Rome really worth, after all? Why did these metal-skirted, sun-tanned soldiers from Italy want to humiliate hitherto friendly Celtic warriors?

Prasutagus was a man of peace, anxious to have things smoothed over without too much fuss. But Boudica was proud

*Dio Cassius, lxi, 3 (p. 23).

and hot-blooded. Her sense of outrage was ever quick to be stirred. Perhaps it was her anger that made the Iceni leaders call together the warriors, and discuss whether they should rise in revolt. Ostorius's best troops were away in the west chasing Caratacus in Wales, and it was a good opportunity for rebellion. The Iceni leaders persuaded some neighbouring tribes to join them, including probably the Trinovantes. Somewhere in East Anglia, in south Norfolk, or on the edge of the Fens, they threw up an earth rampart and cut a deep ditch round a good, flat plain for battle, made the entrance very narrow so that cavalry could not ride through except in single file, and challenged the occupying army to besiege them.* Ostorius is thought to have commanded the Roman force of infantry and what Tacitus called dismounted cavalrymen. The signal was given and the Romans rushed the ramparts, clambered over and fought a desperate hand-to-hand battle with the rebel army inside. The rebels' chosen field now became a trap from which they themselves could not escape.

The defeat of the disaffected Iceni was sharp and decisive. It discouraged other tribes from following them into rebellion. But it also hardened a sense of grievance among the Iceni, and this was to be recalled when, thirteen years later, they rose in revolt again. Prasutagus was spared because he was not involved: he had kept out of the fighting.

It seems that Prasutagus was given extra powers by Ostorius, for after this revolt, he was the only king of the Iceni. Moreover, Prasutagus was popular with the Iceni and his new status had been acceptable to them. This enabled Ostorius to return to the west to hunt down Caratacus, confident that he would not be attacked from the rear.

We do not know how Boudica felt about the collapse of the Icenian rising. Had she been involved in the fighting? Probably not, but only because in 47 she was either still carrying or had recently given birth to her second daughter. Nor do we know any more of the next twelve years of her life with Prasutagus, even where she lived in Norfolk. But there have been enough archaeological remains discovered to let us make one or two guesses.

At the time of the Roman invasion, the Iceni occupied Norfolk and some parts of East Cambridgeshire and High Suffolk. The Catuvellauni had for some time been pressing upon their southern and south-western frontiers, especially in

*The site of Stonea Camp, on an island in the Cambridgeshire Fens between Ely and March, is confidently suggested as a candidate.

the Breckland district. They had also overrun areas of Trinovantian territory in Essex and lower Suffolk and had even
taken over their capital, Camulodunon. The Iceni withdrew
northwards and north-eastwards, possibly to a number of towns
and forts built by them or their ancestors and still occupied by
their kinsmen. There were at least three distinct parts, the
north west coastal area between Hunstanton and Wells-next-
the-Sea, the Norwich area, and the Breckland area around
Thetford. At one time the Iceni constituted two, or maybe
three, tribes, each with a royal house and an area of authority.

At Snettisham, in west Norfolk, a considerable amount of
very rich metalwork, dating from the first century B.C., has
been discovered since 1948. The first objects were found by a
farmer. They included more than fifty gold, silver and bronze
torcs (bracelets and necklets), rings of gold and other metals, a
hoard suggesting the presence of a ruler of great wealth, and
therefore great power, in north Norfolk. This seems to have
been borne out by discoveries of similarly rich metal objects,
though not in the same quantities, nearby at Bawsey, North
Creake and Ringstead. But discoveries have also been made in
east-central Norfolk. A hill fort was found at Tasburgh, about
seven miles south of Norwich, and this could have been a
centre of the eastern Iceni. Pottery of the first century B.C. has
been found nearby which would support the presence of Iron
Age British in the area.

In Breckland, meanwhile, a number of discoveries show the
first century A.D. dominion of the Catuvellauni over the Iceni,
from finds at Snailwell near Newmarket (including a grave in
which there was a couch ornamented with bronze plates), at
Elveden (pottery and bronze objects). A few miles further to
the north-east at Thetford, the remains of an Icenian earthwork
were found jumbled up with the remains of a later Norman
motte-and-bailey castle of the eleventh century. Possibly it
had been a fort thrown up at the time of the Catuvellaunian
advance, but see below (pp. 59-61) for A. K. Gregory's recent
excavations at Gallows Hill, north-west Thetford.

The Romans took steps to prevent further disturbances in
the land of the Iceni by fencing them in, as it were, with a
military road and some forts. The road, now known as Peddars
Way, ran from the extreme north-west of Norfolk down in a
south-easterly sweep to Breckland and as far as Ixworth.
Peddars Way crosses the Wissey river near North Pickenham,

I. A possible reconstruction of an early Iron Age house at West Harling, Norfolk, as portrayed in a model in Norwich Castle Museum.

II. A reconstruction of a large Iron Age house, perhaps of the type occupied by a Celtic lord, based on excavations at Pimperne in Dorset. The completed house was built at the Butser Iron Age Farm in Hampshire.

III & IV. An Iron Age gold alloy torc, above, found at Bawsey in Norfolk and now in the C Museum at Norwich. This could be the kind of torc worn by Boudica. Below are coir Prasutagus, Boudica's husband.

ilip II of Macedon stater (1)

Gallo-Belgic A stater (2)

Gallo-Belgic E stater (5)

Early Icenian stater (7)

evelopment of the horse
n on Celtic gold coins,
e, derived from Greek
els. 1. Stater of Philip II
acedon (fourth century
); 2. Gallo-Belgic A
r (second century B.C.);
allo-Belgic E stater (first
ry B.C.); 4. Early Iceni
r (c. 10 B.C.-c. A.D. 20).

The celebrated statue of
lica and her daughters
homas Thornycroft on
orth end of Westminster
ge, right.

Model of a British war
ot, below, based on the
of Sir Cyril Fox at Llyn
ig Bach, Anglesey.

VIII. An aerial photograph of the site of the Iron Age palace at Gallows Hill, Thetford, before excavations began under the direction of A. K. Gregory. The breaks in the lines (centre right) indicate entrances facing east.

IX. An aerial photograph of the site at Gallows Hill, Thetford, after stripping of the surface soil. The three circular houses can be faintly seen in the enclosure at centre right, in line top to bottom (north to south) near the western double ditch. (Norfolk Archaeological unit photograph)

X. The tombstone of Longinus Sdapezama-
tygus, a Moesian auxiliary who had served in
Britain. .He is portrayed trampling on a
fallen enemy, possibly a Briton. The Roman's
face has been smashed, but the Briton's
portrait is unharmed. The tombstone was
damaged during the assault on Colchester;
was the Briton's face left undefaced on
purpose? This stone is now in the Colchester
and Essex Museum.

XI. Part of the wall of a house in the *coloni*
at Colchester destroyed in the assault. Not
the socket holes for the burnt-out timbe
and the smaller wattles of the wattle-and
daub construction. This discovery was mad
during excavations at Lion Walk by th
Colchester Archaeological Trust.

XII. An aerial photograph of the earthworks at Stonea Camp, Cambridgeshire, which might be the Iron Age fort attacked by Ostorius Scapula in A.D. 47/48.

XIII. What was possibly the final battlefield, seen from the Roman position. This is a ridge south of Watling Street at Mancetter. The Roman army was protected by a wood behind it and on two sides, and had a dominating view northwards over the Boudican forces in the south of Swaffham. About two miles east of this crossing, at a place called Ashill, is an irregular rectangular enclosure on rising ground, about 250 feet above sea level. The site overlooks the river crossing. There was a surrounding ditch and bank, and there is evidence that a Roman fort could have been erected there either after the 47 revolt or after Boudica's rebellion. It might, alternatively, have been an Icenian structure to meet the threat of Roman forces during either of the revolts, or even one put up during Prasutagus's rule from 47 to 59.*

Within the area bounded by Peddars Way the Iceni lived at peace for the rest of Prasutagus's reign. Where he and Boudica held court we do not know, but the site at Tasburgh and the pottery finds nearby to the north at Caistor St Edmunds suggest it could have been in the Norwich district. Soon after the collapse of Boudica's rebellion the Romans built a town at Caistor St Edmunds. There is nothing so far to show that this town was erected on the remains of a British town, but its geographical location, which attracted the Romans, may also have appealed to the Iceni.

Prasutagus and Boudica concentrated upon the development of agriculture. Tacitus described Prasutagus as having been a man of great wealth, by which he meant not merely material possessions but farming wealth, too.† Norfolk has always been one of the best districts in all Britain for farming. In the last few centuries it has been famous for the abundance and quality of its corn. In Prasutagus's time pasturing sheep and cattle would probably have been the main use of the land. Britain was already exporting wool to the Continent. The ownership of cattle and sheep was a status symbol in Celtic society. But that is not to understate the contribution made by corn growing. Caesar commented upon the scale of it in southern Britain in the first century B.C. And there must have been a lot of export business in corn. Some of Cunobelinus's coins carry a barley ear on one side, which was an advertisement of a major industry.

Prasutagus would sometimes have been paid for his products in hard cash, but he might also have received other commodities in exchange, including perhaps iron utensils and weapons, jars and flagons of wine, and so forth. Such wealth

*The Enclosure at Ashill; A. K. Gregory, Norfolk Archaeology, 1976, pp. 9-30.

†Tacitus, Annals, xiv. 31.

excited the envious eyes of some of the financial officers of the
Roman government at Camulodunum, and how they tried to
get their hands on it after Prasutagus's death was a major
cause of the great rebellion.

The Iceni began soon enough to learn what it was really like
to be under Roman sovereignty. A client-kingship of independence was shown to be an empty phrase. It was the Roman
custom when granting client-kingships to limit their duration
to the lifetime of the first holder. Thereafter, the "kingdom"
would be absorbed into the Roman orbit and brought under
the direct control of the provincial administration, with all
that that meant.

The system of government introduced in Britain in 43 was
the same as that in the other provinces of the empire. The
emperor appointed a governor, or legatus, from the ranks of
the Senate. Usually, he had been a consul at Rome at some
time. He was responsible for both civil and military administration and was commander-in-chief of the imperial armed
forces in the province (which consisted of both army and naval
units). The finances of the province, however, were in the
hands of another imperial officer, the procurator. As a rule he
was chosen from a lower class of people, the equites, or
businessmen's class (outside the Senate). Each of the officials
was expected to keep an eye on the possible excesses of the
other. This often meant, however, that the two reached a sort
of agreement to keep out of each other's spheres of influence,
the opposite of what was intended.

If the province or district was directly governed by the
Roman legatus, and the finances managed by the procurator,
then the burdens on the native people were heavy. There were
many different taxes; land tax, property tax (a different
thing), customs dues, imposts on agricultural products, and
more. The native people also had to contribute to the cost of
the "privilege" of having Roman occupying forces in their
land. This was a severe drain on local resources, and many
people found they had to borrow money. There were always
plenty of Romans willing to act as moneylenders at high
interest rates for themselves or on behalf of rich investors in
Italy or elsewhere who sought a good income return on their
capital wealth invested in another province. If the administration of tax collecting and the supervision of money-lending
activities were in the hands of a firm and honest procurator,

then the burdens were just about bearable. But when in about 57 a new procurator, Catus Decianus, was sent to Britain, the province got a taste of Roman harshness and corruption at its worst. As we shall see, it was the policy carried out by Catus on the death of Prasutagus that finally drove the Iceni into revolt.

The financial hardships were not the only burdens. The legatus could conscript native men for the armies (and very often did). He could force people into work on road building and other civil engineering projects, under slave overseers. He could commandeer supplies of corn and food for his troops, and order farmers to yield up cattle or other livestock. He could demand a tax to pay for special building projects, over and above the other imposts. The Trinovantes, for example, were forced to contribute to the construction of the temple of Claudius at Camulodunum, and also to provide much of the manpower for the actual building work.

How much of these numerous burdens was borne by the Iceni we do not know. They were supposed by their special relationship with Rome to be exempt or nearly exempt from them, but their independence did not stop Roman troops or administrative officials from wandering about Norfolk more or less at will. Nor did it prevent individual acts of extortion by corrupt officials, accompanied by armed troops, perhaps, to make their work easier. Tacitus says that the British felt that whereas each tribe had previously had one chief, now, under Rome, two were set over them, the legatus and procurator, the former wielding tyrannical power over their persons, the latter over their property.*

Relations between Prasutagus and Boudica and the Roman administration were probably smooth. The Romans could afford to be pleasant. Prasutagus was rich. He had already made his will, in which he left half his wealth to the emperor Nero and the other half to his two daughters. By including the emperor he hoped to guarantee that the remainder would reach his heirs. His kingdom, he knew very well, would pass into direct Roman rule on his death; that is what happened to all client-kingships. The Romans for their part could wait. Meanwhile, a popular rule, friendly to Rome, was keeping his people on the right side of the law.

It is tantalizing to speculate on the relationship between Prasutagus and Boudica. It is hard not to have the impression of an older man, kindly, generous, soft-hearted, easily taken

*Tacitus, *Agricola*, xv (p. 65).

BOUDICA

in, anxious for peace at any price, perhaps an admirer of the
Roman way of life, married quite happily to a young woman,
very different from himself, fiery, impatient, unwilling to
suffer fools, suspicious, sharply intelligent, cunning when
necessary, very proud of her race, her descent and her royal
dignity, and sceptical of the Romans and all that they stood
for. Boudica would not have seen them as civilizers, as bringers
of a better way of life. To her they were greedy, grasping,
violent, humourless, brutal and self-aggrandizing, interested
only in pleasure, acquisition and military oppression. She
would have studied history, known of the long catalogue of
nations overcome by Rome which had suffered almost to the
point of extinction, certainly to the loss of national identity.
She might have learned of it from the Druids.

A word should be said about the Druids. They were the
priests in Celtic society. They were generally responsible for
education and they were guardians of the law. Although they
may have been able to write things down, they chose to
communicate and to teach by word of mouth. They taught by
means of poetry, not so much the rhyming verse we understand
today but the musical rhythm of the words or syllables of words
which could — and can — be imprinted upon the memory by
listening and repeating several times. The range of things they
taught was wide, and included history (some of it perhaps
confused with legend), simple science (such as astronomy,
physics, geography), and religion and law. By limiting their
lessons to oral ones, they maintained considerable secrecy
about their sources of knowledge and their activities, to such
an extent that even today relatively little is known about them.
This reticence gave them great power and influence.

Boudica will have been fully aware of this power, manifest
at that time in Wales where they were the mainstay of Celtic
resistance to the Romans. She and her husband may have
allowed Druids to reside and teach in Norfolk, to preach and
keep alive the spirit of Celtic nationalism there. She may have
permitted some of the more frightful ceremonies and rituals,
including human sacrifice,* which these weird fanatics practised, which had been noted by Caesar in his account of the
conquest of Gaul. He thought that druidical teaching had
originated in Britain. He also noted that the Druids had no
fear of death. They believed in the immortality of the soul.
The soul moved into another body. The fact of their belief in

*Some of the barbarities inflicted on the Roman settlers at Colchester and
London during her revolt must be explained by the survival of Druidical
influence among her followers.

the after-life has been borne out by archaeological finds of graves "richly furnished with this world's wealth". The in-difference to death gave Celts a frantic courage, especially in defeat.

In the last years of Prasutagus's reign, grievances were building up among the subject peoples in Britain. There was the harsh and corrupt financial manipulating of Catus Decianus, there were the unremitting taxes, the arrogance of the Roman military and the colonists who had started to make Britain their permanent home. Then, in 58, a new legatus arrived. He was Gaius Suetonius Paullinus. His military policies combined with the procurator's oppressiveness to provoke the outbreak of a frightful rebellion.

CHAPTER FIVE

The Revolt Breaks Out

THE defeat of Caratacus in 51 did not lead to the collapse of British resistance in mid- and north Wales. The unbeaten tribes there regarded it merely as a setback from which they should be spurred on to continue the struggle. They were encouraged by the Druids, whose headquarters were in Mona (Anglesey), and who were still exerting considerable religious influence among the Celts generally to keep alive the fierce hatred of all things Roman.

The reckless courage of the Celts and their indifference to death still had to be reckoned with, and the Romans found the task of subduing Wales very much more difficult than they had calculated. The legatus, Quintus Veranius, who took up his post in 57, had been confident of winning Wales in a two-year, or at the most three-year, campaign, but he died in 58, leaving his successor Suetonius Paullinus with the great part of the country and the island of Anglesey still unconquered.

Gaius Suetonius Paullinus was probably in his sixties, with a long career of military service to his credit. Only a year or so before Aulus Plautius came across to Britain in 43, Suetonius was winning fame as governor of Mauretania (now Morocco and Algeria). He led his legions over the High Atlas mountains and crushed the tribesmen who had been raiding Roman positions in the province for some years. It had been a decisive victory achieved in very quick time. He returned to Rome to well-earned honours and was made consul. Then he disappears from history for about fifteen years. During that time, however, Suetonius cannot have been inactive for long. It is reasonable to surmise that he held other commands. And when Emperor Nero needed a replacement for Quintus Veranius, one who could carry out the conquest of Wales, he picked Suetonius because of his experience of mountain warfare.

On reaching Britain in 58/9 Suetonius looked at the position in great detail. He calculated that to undertake the conquest of Wales, he would need at least two legions. Available were Legio XIV and Legio XX, and he could call upon detachments from the other legions, together with auxiliaries, which would make up a force of perhaps 20,000 men. This army, together with its equipment, artillery and supplies, would have to be moved across unconquered tracts of midland Britain. Most of the territory was in friendly hands, but it would still be a massive operation. Then the army would have to establish a base at a site suitable for an advance into northern Wales.

Suetonius decided upon a site at Chester (Deva), then probably no more than a village, which had a good harbour on the river Dee. A fort was built, and a road was begun that would join up with Fosse Way. From Chester, Suetonius would launch a two-pronged offensive westwards, one along the coastal flats north of the Snowdon mountain range to northern Caernarvonshire, and the other along the southern side of the mountains and through to the west coast. When north Wales had been overcome by these encircling movements, he would then invade Anglesey, destroy the centre of druidism and round up the remaining Celtic fighters for freedom. He hoped this would frighten the rest of Wales into submission, but in the event, the conquest of Wales was not completed until the late 70s, under Julius Agricola, governor from 78 to 84.

Militarily speaking, at the time the strategy was sound. The Brigantes in the northern midlands and Yorkshire were still a client-kingdom under their queen, Cartimandua. Below the Fosse Way the province was quiet. Suetonius reckoned he could leave everything to local administrations. The new *colonia* at Camulodunum was being built, with temple, meeting house and theatre, by a seemingly cooperative labour force of Trinovantian workers. The financial affairs of the province were in what he believed to be the capable hands of Catus Decianus. It seemed safe to tackle the Welsh problem. So he ordered the troop columns to move forwards towards Chester.

The campaign in Wales turned out only partly as Suetonius planned. It took two winters to overcome resistance in the mainland of north Wales, but, as Tacitus put it, he subdued various nations (that is, tribes) and established garrisons, which entailed the construction of forts. This inspired him to prepare for the invasion of Anglesey. There, the Druids had ordained that the Celts should make their last stand against

Roman imperialism. If the Celts could not turn the Romans back, then they would meet on the field whatever fate was in store for them. And so it came to pass: "Onward pressed the Roman standards and they bore down their opponents, enveloping them in the flames of their own torches. Suetonius then garrisoned the conquered island."* He demolished the sacred groves of oak trees in which the Druids practised their frightful ceremonies, and in doing so it is said that every oak tree in the island was torn from its seat and burned. Today it is practically impossible to find an oak in Anglesey. "The fires of fanaticism were stamped out by hobnail boots", wrote Professor Dudley. Druidism was dead: its influence was brought to an end, the Romans thought.

Suetonius and his senior officers were congratulating each other and the troops celebrating victory when despatch riders on fast horses arrived at the commander-in-chief's tent, bearing the most shattering news. The Iceni had risen in revolt in Norfolk, other tribes had joined them, and under the leadership of the fiery queen Boudica, a vast throng of some 100,000 angry British warriors, and the wives and families of many of them, had tramped down the eastern side of East Anglia to Colchester. There, in a vigorous assault, they had in two days taken the town, set it on fire, destroyed the great proportion of its new buildings, including the temple of Claudius, and butchered almost the entire colony of Roman settlers and officials, probably as many as 20,000 people. Flushed with her success, Boudica was planning to turn westwards, head for Caesaromagus (Chelmsford) and make for London or St Albans, the messengers did not know which.

The revolt was a major disaster for the Romans. It took Suetonius completely by surprise. During his absence in Wales he had been receiving regular intelligence reports of the situation throughout the rest of the province. Roman military and political intelligence was the most highly organised the world had seen. As a rule there was not much about his province and its subjects that was kept from a provincial governor. Quite often they got to hear of revolts even before they had moved beyond the planning stage. But this revolt had achieved one of its major objectives before the governor had heard anything.

Even before the arrival of Suetonius in Britain, there were enough grievances to generate revolt. From the first days of his

*Tacitus, *Annals*, xiv. 30, (p. 317).

appointment Catus Decianus had begun to make himself hated for his greed and for the brutality with which he raised taxes. Even a Roman historian (Tacitus) put the blame on Catus for what happened. His rapacity had driven the province to war. Things came to a head when old Prasutagus died in 59. Everyone knew he had made Nero joint heir to his personal fortune. This included farms, homesteads, cattle, sheep, corn stores, and, probably, cash and valuables. Everyone also know that on his death his client-kingship would end and Iceni territory would come under Roman rule. What the Iceni did not expect was that Catus would now say that the grants of land and sums of money originally authorised by Claudius in 43 to many of the British nobility, and not intended to be recoverable by Rome, were now revoked, that is, they had to be paid back after all and probably with accumulated interest. Dio Cassius recorded that the philosopher Seneca, tutor and later adviser to Nero, had invested the equivalent of many thousands of pounds (about 40,000,000 sesterces) in loans to British chiefs and landowners, and now suddenly he called them all in, becoming very unpleasant indeed when they were not repaid promptly.* Doubtless Catus used official collectors to enforce these repayments of private loans, as well as repayment of Claudius's grants.

Catus's treasury agents, accompanied by greedy soldiers looking for loot, went systematically through Iceni territory demanding money or title-deeds, and sometimes both. A posse of them arrived at the palace of Prasutagus, which may have been near Norwich,† where the royal clerks were making lists of the late king's possessions. They barged in unannounced and went straight to Boudica. Probably one of them insulted her, while others paid unwelcome attentions to her two daughters. Boudica will have risen at once to this. She may have slapped the face of the first Roman. Whatever it was, she was taken outside and fastened to a stake where the soldiers flogged her. At the same time, her daughters began screaming as other soldiers chased them along the passage to their bedroom where the two young girls were assaulted and raped.

It was one of the most frightful outrages the Romans ever perpetrated during the centuries of their association with Britain. News of the atrocities spread like wildfire throughout Norfolk. In every town and village, farm and hamlet, people

*Dio Cassius, lxii, 2, (p. 83).

†Or was it at Gallow's Hill, near Thetford (see pp. 59-61).

heard of it with horror. Many people knew Boudica, many more knew about her. Her courage and leadership were admired everywhere. By many she was regarded as a goddess. When her husband Prasutagus died, his people had elected her to rule in his place. It was natural to turn to Boudica.

A flogging at the hands of the Roman soldiery was no light matter. They would not have spared their strength because of Boudica's sex. To them she was a barbarian. Her daughters, probably no older than 15 and 14, respectively, would have been even worse used, and the shock and suffering from such an assault must have driven them to the edge of collapse. But their mother was a brave woman and a tough one, and she quickly threw aside her anguish and humiliation. In their place welled up all the anger for which the highly-strung Celts have always been well known. And when she was angry, all Icenia was angry, too. Here was a people united now, outraged, their souls filled with resentment. Surely the time had come to rise. Whatever Boudica decided to do to avenge the outrage, clearly her people would rally behind her.

The grievances of the Iceni are thus easy to understand. But how did Boudica get the Trinovantes in Essex and East Suffolk to join her? The answer is that she made it her business to find out about the deep-seated and long-held grievances of the Trinovantes against the Romans. She may have been studying them for years. The absence of Suetonius and a large chunk of the Roman army of occupation on campaign in Wales enabled the British in East Anglia to move about a little more freely, and doubtless she had talks with Trinovantian leaders who gave her some first-hand details of the less agreeable features of direct Roman rule.

The Trinovantes had believed that when the Romans defeated the Catuvellauni in Essex, the victors would return to them their old capital of Camulodunon (pp. 19-20). Possibly, one of their chiefs was among the eleven kings who submitted to Claudius. But the Romans had other ideas. The Trinovantes had resisted the Roman advance, albeit under Catuvellaunian compulsion. They had to pay the price. Their lands were treated as conquered soil, and the Romans decided to build a new provincial capital right beside Camulodunon and to found a *colonia* there. What this entailed was planting in their midst a strong body of privileged and often arrogant Roman ex-soldiers who had retired after twenty or twenty-five years' service with a grant of land, a cash sum and allowances in the shape of agricultural tools. Most of the settlers came from Italy where they had been used to living in towns, and the *colonia* was a town of buildings, private and public, with the pieces of land which the settlers had been given to farm outside it. And to provide this land, Trinovantian landholders were dispossessed of their estates. To compensate, if that is the right word, they were pressed into service on a variety of civil engineering works in the *colonia* — roads, buildings, public and private, harbour and temples.

The final insult was the construction of the Temple of Claudius, to be the centre of a new religious cult in Britain, worship of the emperor. The new "religion" was to be served by a high priest and priestess chosen from the upper classes of the surrounding tribes. And the cost of the new cult, including expensive ceremonial, clothing, equipment, and so on, was to be borne in the main by the Trinovantes. Rome was ordering them to pay for a new religion imposed on them, when they had an acceptable one of their own. Here was a potentially dangerous situation, but the Trinovantes did not rebel, because they saw that they could not win against the greatest army in the world. Nor did they conspire with the Iceni, for the Iceni had been allowed to remain independent.

But Trinovantian grievances festered because they were not dealt with. When Boudica made her first tentative approaches, probably while her husband Prasutagus was still alive, some of the Trinovantes saw a glimmer of hope for better times. After her husband's death, she would have used all her skill to identify the Trinovantian cause with her own, more so, after the assault committed on her own person. Here were the ingredients with which to weld together a formidable confederation of East Anglian people. Possibly she obtained promises of support from other neighbouring tribes, including the Coritani and some disaffected Catuvellauni people in the Home Counties.

One of the most remarkable things about the great revolt was the way in which Boudica managed to marshal a huge army in Norfolk, with its chariots, horses and equipment, move it southwards on the road towards Colchester, picking up a large Trinovantian force on the way, probably near the Icenian border, all without attracting the attention of Roman intelligence. There were spies in every British tribe, some of them on the regular payroll of the authorities. And yet, until the first of the forts along Peddars Way was attacked by the forward patrols of Boudica's host, the Romans had no inkling of the danger they were in. Clearly, feeling against Rome was so high that no one was willing to betray the Iceni cause.

Colchester was the obvious first target for the angry host of British people. Apart from the Trinovantian desire for revenge, for the Iceni there was the fact that the men who assaulted Boudica and her daughters, and who came to take away whatever they could of Prasutagus's possessions, had set out from the *colonia*. Perhaps Boudica believed, or even had information, that Catus Decianus, the grasping procurator, was there.*

Sometime in the spring of 61, at about the time Suetonius was preparing to take his army across the Menai Strait from Caernarvonshire to Anglesey, the tribes began to mass in Norfolk. Boudica called a conference of the leaders. We do not know which tribes were represented, apart from the Trinovantes, but there may have been chiefs of the Durotriges of Dorset, the Dobunni of the Cotswolds, the Coritani, and perhaps leaders among disaffected people from Queen Cartimandua's Brigantian kingdom. At the meeting, which may have been on a hill near Caistor St Edmunds, or at Thetford (see pp. 59-61), Boudica harangued the delegates with strong, fiery words, which were summarized by Tacitus.† She told them not to be frightened of the numbers of troops the Romans could send against them. If the tribes would unite, their armies would outnumber the Romans several times. She urged them to remember their ancestors and not to be put off if the first engagement turned out to be a defeat. They could return again and again until victory was won. She swore that the gods themselves were on the British side, and doubtless as she did so, Druid priests raised their arms to the sky and chanted suitable prayers and invocations. She told them to take full advantage of the absence of Suetonius. He was over 200 miles away and it would take three weeks at least for him to bring his army back to East Anglia.

The meeting cheered and clapped. Then the delegates moved forward and saluted Boudica as their leader. They returned to their camps and began to marshal their warriors. Many of the men had pitched their tents in groups in the shelter of woods and copses, and stayed in camp for a night or

*Though when Boudica reached Colchester, Catus had already left for London.

†*Agricola*, xv, (pp. 65-66).

two awaiting the great day on which the march would begin. A day or two later, the whole army, some 120,000 strong, drew up somewhere on the flat plains south of Norwich, perhaps near Long Stratton.* On that day, their leaders put on their finest clothing for the great expedition. Perhaps they wore the sort of clothes that Cuchullain sported in one of his great battles: a well-fitting mantle, purple and in five folds; a tunic of silk, edged with gold or silver braid and fringes, which reached to the top of his dark red satin apron; a deep purple shield, with a rim of white silver round it; and, hanging from his belt a long sword, with a golden ornamented hilt. In the chariot which accompanied him was a long spear and sharp dagger. Diodorus Siculus described some Celtic battle dress: the shields of the principal men were nearly as big as the men themselves; they were beautifully decorated to each individual's favoured style, some with projecting bronze animal motifs, wonderfully carved; their helmets were of bronze, crested on top with animal figures in bronze, and sometimes incorporating horns. These interesting contemporary details are borne out by remains discovered by archaeologists (cf. the iron helmet with bronze crest found at Tordos in Rumania). The helmets made the men seem taller than they really were. They also wore iron breast-plates of chain mail. How many of the British leaders were so magnificently appareled at the time we are speaking about we do not know, but it was a centuries-old custom for leaders to be prominent because of their physical strength and prowess and for these qualities to be advertised to the enemy.

Suddenly, the harsh blare of hunting horns was heard. Boudica was coming to start the great procession. Surrounded by chariots on all four sides, she stood on her own vehicle as she was driven swiftly to a specially raised rostrum. Boldly she stepped on to it, tall, terrifying in her anger, fierce in her eyes, harsh in her voice. A great mass of reddish hair tumbled about her head and down to her waist. Around her neck was the great twisted golden necklace, and over her shoulders a tunic of many colours under a thick woollen cloak fastened with a dazzling brooch. On her forehead was a bright blue tattoo mark.† It was probably the figure of a single human eye—

---

*But see pp. 59-61. If Gallows Hill was Boudica's headquarters, then the host probably assembled in the fields now occupied by Thetford, and set off towards Colchester.

†Some years ago, the bodies of some Scythians (from whom the Celts stemmed) were found preserved in ice and snow in Siberia. They were getting on for 3000 years old. Bluish tattoo marks were discernible on some of them, and this could be where the Celts derived the idea.

watching, rivetting the gaze of all who looked upon her. She held a huge spear, and as she spoke she shook it, twirled it about and mesmerized those standing before her. Then she spoke—at some length, according to Dio Cassius.* She reminded them that they had once been free and had now tasted of slavery. She stressed the onerous tax impositions inflicted year after year. She told them that they—all of them, including herself—were in part responsible for these evils because they did not throw back the Romans when the latter arrived in Kent in 43. Now they could remedy the situation, especially as they were united, had so much on their side—an abundance of bravery, ability to hide in swamps and mountains and elude the enemy, capacity to survive on the toughest of diets of grass and roots, juice and water, intimate knowledge of the terrain. "Let us go against them, trusting to good fortune. Let us show them that they are hares and foxes trying to rule over dogs and wolves."

Then—Forward! And the word in its Celtic equivalent spread back down the lines, and the army began to move. Jumbled up in the columns were the wives and children of many of the warriors, some with four-wheel carts carrying their possessions, offerings for the gods, food and spare weapons and armour, while flanking the great columns on both sides were hundreds of chariots, the lightweight two-wheeled kind we have described above (p. 13). Onward moved the host, making at the most ten miles a day. As it came to the Roman outpost at Scole it swept down past it, though possibly the queen detached a force to chase and cut down the small Roman contingent there. Over at Ashill, other British tribes, on the march to join with the main columns, probably overran the Roman fort and continued down Peddars Way to meet Boudica somewhere in Suffolk, perhaps at Baylham, near Coddenham.

On the fourth or fifth day, the tribes had all joined up and the host, said by Dio Cassius to have numbered 120,000, but probably nearer to 100,000, was about 20 miles from the first objective—Colchester. This *colonia* of about 20,000 Roman settlers, their wives and children, officials, troops and a population of British subject people living and working there, some under duress, some willingly, was to have forewarning of its fate. The town authorities had been over-confident. Instead of surrounding the site with a strong protective wall and ditch,

*Dio Cassius, lxii. 3-5, (pp. 85-91).

with stout gates, they had spent their time and resources on the Claudian temple and other public buildings and civilian amenities. They thought they were safe. Suddenly, according to Tacitus, the statue of Victory "with its back turned as though it were fleeing the enemy" fell down. Frantic women, some of them perhaps influenced by druids or by agents of Boudica, went about singing dirge-like songs of doom and destruction to come. Weird yells and groans were heard in the assembly hall and were in an eerie way echoed in the theatre. Reports ran wild that the sea by the harbour had turned red. Bodies had been seen washed up on the shore.*

Some of the settlers became seriously alarmed, as well they might, and they began to make preparations to defend Colchester. Spades and picks were fetched and a start was made on a ditch and rampart to encircle it. But as they began, some of the native residents rushed round telling them not to pay any attention to the portents. They did not mean anything. The Romans were confused. One of their senior men sent messengers to Catus Decianus, the procurator, who had already gone to London, to report the fears of the residents and to ask for help. Catus responded by sending a token force of about 200 men, but these were not properly armed. Taking this reinforcement into account, the local authorities could barely muster 1,000 armed men to defend themselves. And then, as the leaders considered what they should do, advance units of Boudica's army appeared on the outskirts. At once they began to encircle the *colonia*.

Meanwhile, news of the great march had reached the Roman commander of Legio IX, Quintus Petillius Cerealis, who was at Longthorpe with part of the legion. Probably it was brought by men who had escaped from one of the forts along Peddars Way. Cerealis responded at once, mustered his vexillation of about 2,000 men, infantry and cavalry mixed, and set out for Colchester. The route he took may be guessed. Ermine Street ran from Lincoln to London. He picked up the main road at Water Newton, near Peterborough, went south towards Godmanchester, near Huntingdon, and somewhere along the way he ran straight into an ambush set up by British forces sent by Boudica to meet him. A fierce battle followed, and the Roman infantry was cut to pieces. Petillius Cerealis fled from the field with such cavalry as had survived, with difficulty made his way back to Longthorpe and shut himself

*Tacitus, *Annals*, xiv. 32, (p. 318).

behind the legionary fortress gates. Colchester was now completely isolated. Boudica could do what she liked with it — and she destroyed it.

When the main host of Boudica's warriors had reached the city, the defenders knew that all was lost. The small force with arms fled to the Temple of Claudius, the only building strong enough to withstand fire, and made ready to fight it out. The many thousands who were unarmed were left to shift for themselves — and they did not get far. The *colonia* was set on fire and it went up in flames rapidly, as most of the buildings were made of wood. Within a day it was almost burned to the ground, and only the temple remained. The British besieged the temple, shooting flaming arrows into the roof, and after two days desperate fighting, it fell. What followed has been engraved on the pages of the history of Roman Britain as a dreadful example of Celtic vengeance. No one was spared, neither child nor old person, neither cripple nor pregnant woman. Those who were killed on the spot were fortunate. Those who were not were taken away and subjected to every kind of outrage. "All this they did to the accompaniment of sacrifices, banquets and wanton behaviour", said Dio Cassius, after describing some of the more revolting atrocities.

More than 1,900 years afterwards, excavations in Colchester have revealed evidence of the sack of the *colonia* by Boudica. Burnt clay, sherds, melted glass and shattered oil lamps, all showing signs of subjection to great heat, have been found on sites in the present High Street.* The destruction seems to have been thorough and purposeful. A tombstone of a junior Roman officer carrying a relief sculpture of him on a horse, trampling upon a fallen Briton, was smashed. The officer's face was destroyed, but the face of the Briton was left untouched (see Plate X).

Dio Cassius also tells us that some of the Roman captives were rounded up for a special fate, a slow sacrificial death in what he called the sacred grove of Andate. He says Andate is another word for Victory,† Andate may, on the other hand, be another rendering of Andarta, a goddess of the Vocontii tribe which occupied south-east Gaul. The meaning may be "the invincible", and perhaps Boudica and her victorious troops had decided to offer up these victims to the goddess who had brought the Britons victory. It was customary for the Celts to offer the gods a token collection of the skulls of the defeated.

Camulodunum, by Joan and David Clarke, Ginn & Co. 1971.

† Dio Cassius, lxii. 7, (p. 95).

Boudica had fulfilled the first of her ambitions. It was a dramatic achievement. The whole Roman regime in Britain stood in danger of collapse. The great queen seemed unstoppable. Catus Decianus, meanwhile, had been informed about the fall of Colchester, and of the size of Boudica's host. The news horrified him, and he had good cause for alarm. He was the most hated Roman in the province. The Britons were bound to be out to get him, and he did not relish enduring any of the reprisals he had heard about. So he bolted, took ship from London straight to Gaul, and disappeared from the scene.

Back in Colchester, Boudica considered her position. The initiative lay with her for the moment. News of the descent on the *colonia* had reached Suetonius in Wales, hardly a day or two after the *colonia* was sacked. He had reacted swiftly and with cool, considered judgment. Colchester was beyond help, and no one from Wales could get there in time to rescue any of the inhabitants, and in any case he did not have enough detailed information on the strength of Boudica's army. But he could try to anticipate what she might do next. He reasoned thus: British vengeance was being directed against Roman administration and against British people who had collaborated; there were other vulnerable towns, particularly London and St Albans; the two were about the same distance from Colchester (London, c.60, St Albans c.65). Which of the two would Boudica choose to attack first? Suetonius decided that, whichever it was, he could probably get there before her and intercept her army. The journey ought not to take him more than three or four days of hard riding, whereas it would take her more than a week. So he headed for London, taking his cavalry with him. Legio XIV and part of Legio XX, and the auxiliaries he had in Wales, were ordered to set out behind him at once, in the direction of London. They were to follow the Watling Street route. It would take them at least ten days to cover the 250-odd miles. By the time they reached the Midlands inside the first week, say, Northamptonshire or Leicestershire, he would have reached London and sized up the position. But whatever he did, it was Boudica's turn to move.

Boudica decided to attack London. Although it was not a settlement of *colonia* or *municipium* status, London had already become the biggest town in Britain. Its position, safely tucked away among the serpentine coils of the Thames, gave it a measure of defensiveness from attack by sea and at the same time made it a good base for merchant and business activities because of its harbours for trading ships to and from the continent. A prosperous community was already growing up there. Main Roman roads began or finished there, especially Watling Street and Ermine Street. If it was strategically important to the Romans, it would be no less important to Boudica, who may have decided to make it the centre of a new Celtic British kingdom once the Romans had been driven out. But for that, all traces of Romanization must be wiped out, and with them must go those who had thrown in their lot with Rome, the collaborators. The people of London could expect no mercy once she arrived.

A few days after the festivities celebrating the destruction of Colchester were over, the queen led her great army out along the route to Chelmsford (Caesaromagus) and on to London. How long the march took we do not know, but probably ten days or so allowing for stops.

The intentions and movements of Suetonius, meanwhile, will have been of the greatest concern to the queen. She was aware that her own movements were being watched and reported to the Roman governor on his way down to the south, as indeed his progress was likewise being communicated to her. She knew very well that Suetonius, with his small force of fast cavalry, though much farther from London and St Albans than she was, could get to either town before her. London was the obvious first choice, but she was also bent on an assault on St Albans. The town had been favoured by the Romans, it was fast becoming romanised, and there were many Catuvellaunian nationals working for the conquerors and receiving benefits from their collaboration. These men and their families would have to pay the price.

It was Suetonius who reached London first, probably two or three days before Boudica. By this time he had received detailed reports of her host, its strength and its mood. He had no illusions as to the balance of forces; he was completely outnumbered. On his way down from Wales he had sent messengers to the commander of Legio II at Exeter, instructing him to send reinforcements, but the commander was away. The officer in charge, Poenius Postumus, considered it too risky to spare the troops for the march to meet him that

Suetonius had ordered. When Suetonius got to London, it did not take long for him to decide that it would have to be abandoned to Boudica. The scale of the revolt was such that he would only be able to crush it with a decisive victory over her host in the field of battle — on a field of his choice — and not in or around any urban area. For this he needed to meet Legio XIV and Legio XX trudging on their way down Watling Street. Then hopefully, he could draw Boudica towards him and turn upon her.

Suetonius toured London quickly and let it be known that there was nothing he could do for the inhabitants. Those who cared to follow him out of the town were free to do so, but he could not wait to help the old, the sick, the children. Their leaders pleaded with him, but he hardened his heart and brushed them aside. Then he set out, taking with him those who were ready to come.

Boudica reached the outskirts of the east end of the town, probably somewhere not far from the site of the present Tower of London, about a day or two later. The town was as undefended and easy to plunder as Colchester, and the men of her host moved in to enjoy it with relish. Tacitus says they headed for those places where the loot was richest.* Merchants' houses, exchanges and markets were probably the first to be raided and cleaned out of everything of any value. No quarter was given to anyone: no prisoners were taken. The entire population of perhaps some 20,000 was put to death; throats were cut, people were hanged, crucified or burned, according to the whims of their captors. Then the town itself was set on fire and burned down. Excavations at Spitalfields † have revealed a heap of skeletons that, it has been suggested, could represent a cartload or two of victims of the sack.

With London destroyed and all the East Anglian and possibly many other tribes behind her, Boudica was ready to move on. Her aim — and that of her 100,000 supporters — was one major step nearer achievement. As she set out for St Albans, she almost dared Suetonius to stop her.

*   *   *   *

Early in 1981, acting upon an aerial photograph (see picture VIII) of what appeared to be the site of a Roman camp.

*Tacitus, *Annals*, xiv. 33, (p. 319).

†R. G. Collingwood & J. N. L. Myres: *Roman Britain and the English Settlements*. Oxford University Press. 1968 impression.

taken by chance by the Suffolk Aerial Photographic Unit while flying over the undeveloped part of the Fison Way Industrial Estate on Gallows Hill in N.W. Thetford, A. K. Gregory, field officer with the Norfolk Archaeological Unit, cut a trial trench. Preliminary evidence suggested late first century A.D. occupation. Then, with assistance from DoE and employing young people in a Manpower Services Commission Youth Opportunities Project, Tony Gregory directed the stripping of some six acres inside a larger 11-acre defended site. This revealed much interesting data. The site appeared to have had two separate occupations. To the north, there was an Iron Age occupation, probably mid-first century B.C. to early first century A.D. A mould for Iron Age Belgic coins was found, and also three silver Iceni coins.

Beside the Iron Age area — and overlapping part of it — was an early strongly-defended Romano-British rectangular site, described by Tony Gregory as of "noble, even royal significance". Sherds of pottery date its occupation approximately between 47 and 61 A.D., that is, pre-Boudican revolt. The site consisted of an outer ditch about 12 feet wide, 5 feet deep (backfilled probably after 61); within the outer ditch, a second (middle) ditch, 22 feet wide, 7 feet deep (backfilled); and within that an inner enclosure surrounded by a ditch 8 feet wide, 4 feet deep (backfilled). The space between the outer and middle ditches was about 100 feet wide. The inner enclosure covered about one acre, with a gateway in its eastern side.

The rectangular "ring" between outer and middle ditches was filled with timber slots, about 6 inches square, set about one foot apart, in rows about 10 feet apart. These were for timber stakes, positioned obliquely. About 10,000 stakes had been erected in the "ring", indicating a major engineering job requiring substantial labour, to build a massive system of obstacles that was raised as much to impress, to emphasise status, as to defend.

The inner enclosure appears to have contained in line three circular plan buildings, round houses of about 40 feet diameter, each having the doorway facing east. This is confirmed by post-holes and air photography (see plate VIII). Tony Gregory believes these to have been "royal" apartments.

Was this the palace of Prasutagus, built for him (as sole chief of the Iceni) with Roman help after the Iceni revolt put down by Ostorius, in which Prasutagus had played no part and so had been rewarded? If so, it suggests that the gathering of the tribes after Boudica's call to arms in 61 (see above, p. 52) must have taken place in the plains east of Thetford, and the march towards Colchester proceeded eastwards along the Thetford-Bunwell route to Roudham Heath where Peddar's Way crossed. There the march turned southwards to Coney Weston in Suffolk and then Ixworth, forked left to Bildeston and made its way for the last 15 or so miles across country to Colchester (so far, no road of the period between Bildeston and Colchester has yet been found). Alternatively, the tribes could have taken the Thetford-Bunwell route all the way to the latter, and marched from there to join the Pye Road (Caistor St Edmunds to Colchester) at or near Tasburgh, and swung south along Pye Road via Scole (allowing the tribes to clash with the Roman fort garrison at Scole) and thence directly to Colchester. This does seem a tortuous route for a gathering of 100,000 plus, though the other route is hardly less so. The stretch from Bunwell to Tasburgh is still an inferred and not a certain road.

The Gallows Hill site is a major and exciting discovery, and cogently argues for Prasutagus and Boudica having ruled from the Thetford area (which is much the same as saying from Breckland, a long-held tradition). Though I am inclined still to prefer the gathering to have taken place near Caistor St Edmunds, near a Boudican palace as yet undiscovered, I am — as anyone interested in the Boudica story must be — gripped by the possibilities emerging from Tony Gregory's discovery, which is one of the most dramatic archaeological finds in Britain for a decade or so.

CHAPTER SIX

The Reckoning

ONE would give a great deal to know what was in Boudica's mind as she stood somewhere amid the smoking ruins of London, surveying the destruction wreaked by her host. She could be well satisfied with the results so far of her attempt to root out the foundations of Roman civilization in Britain. She was confident that her next target, St Albans, would prove nearly as easy to deal with as London, for it was not properly fortified either. But what after that? She knew that there was more to making a revolt against an occupying power successful than merely sacking undefended towns. There was the Roman army to contend with, consisting as it still did of some 40,000 of the finest soldiers in the world, even if it was split up into regional commands. Her troops, fighting people of both sexes, had proved effective through their numerical strength and their morale. Some of them had been more than a match for a small Roman force, the detachment from Longthorpe led by Petillius Cerealis. But how would a large army of the Iceni fare in a pitched battle against the Roman commander, one of Rome's best generals, who had already subjugated Boudica's kinsfolk in Wales?

Boudica could be understood for having doubts about her future strategy. The events that immediately followed her sack of London suggest that she decided to avoid a major confrontation with Suetonius. Her assault and sack of St Albans was to be a waste of precious military time, however. A good general would have followed Suetonius — at a discreet distance behind — until he could manoeuvre him into an unfavourable position and compel him to fight at a disadvantage. But Boudica was not a general. She was a leader of an angry and very undisciplined mob, and she had no generals in her entourage. The momentum of her war was carried along by the feeling of hatred for all things Roman, the yearning for vengeance, personified in herself, and by the taste of her followers for loot and blood. It may not be fanciful to suggest that Boudica was revolted and perhaps frightened by some of the excesses of cruelty and murder dealt out to the populations of Colchester, London and St Albans. But she was powerless to stop them. Before long she was to see how this unruly mob failed to cope with the splendidly drilled and determined Roman army in full battle conditions.

Whichever way Suetonius left London, Boudica did not immediately try to catch up with him. Instead, with St Albans now at the top of the vengeance list, she marshalled her host and led it forward some twenty miles north-westwards to the former Catuvellaunian *oppidum*, with its poulation of collaborators, and there her forces broke loose and indulged in a further orgy of fire, pillage and murder. The work of 17 years of Roman-inspired construction was reduced to little more than a heap of ashes. Evidence of the thoroughness of this sack was found by Professor S. S. Frere, whose excavations of the Catuvellaunian site in the 1950s and 1960s are among the most remarkable of all Romano-British archaeological discoveries.*

Boudica's destruction of St Albans gave Suetonius several days' head start in which to meet the legions coming down from Wales and to begin accumulating food supplies, notably corn, for the possibility of several weeks' campaigning. He would have commandeered supplies from farms around the countryside, probably paying for them in some cases, but where there was difficulty in getting farmers to cooperate, he would have appropriated them with imperial authority. As he hastened up into the Midlands, he sent fast riders ahead along Watling Street with orders to the legions that they should not come any further down the great arterial road than the crossroads at High Cross (Venonae) in Leicestershire where it met Fosse Way, or possibly at Wall (Letocetum) in Staffordshire, where Watling Street was crossed by another good road from the south-west. Perhaps he also hoped that the detachments he had sent for from Legio II at Exeter might, after all, have arrived, despite Postumus's disobedience of orders.

By concentrating his forces, with their very much superior mobility and speed, Suetonius was drawing Boudica and her army into the Northamptonshire-Warwickshire area. Accompanied by the wives and children of many of the warriors, and their waggons and carts, her army had to negotiate largely unfamiliar countryside, somewhat less flat and open, peppered

*They are detailed by Professor S. S. Frere in *Verulamium*. Antiquity xxxvi (1956), xlii (1962) and *Verulamium Excavations*, I. O.U.P. 1972.

with areas of forest and hilly woodland. This stretched out her columns for miles and miles, making it extremely difficult for her to keep control. It also slowed them down. Added to that, Boudica could not be sure of the same kind of unquestioning support that she had enjoyed in East Anglia. After all, a good proportion of her victims in St Albans had been British, not Roman, and attempts to swell her ranks by recruiting among the tribes in Buckinghamshire and Bedfordshire hills may have proved unfruitful, since those that had heard about the burning of the town may not have seen matters in the same light as she did.

There were other factors. The Romans had made a considerable impression in the southern Midlands of Britain, where there had been less resistance to the original invasion campaigns. Some of the eleven kings who submitted to Claudius would have come from these parts, and this may be why when, in 43, Caratacus had tried to whip up support for his resistance, his negotiations in the Midlands fell flat, thus compelling him to seek allies further westwards. Suetonius was brought up in the tradition of Roman imperial policies, one of which was that in lands just annexed to the empire, which were composed of several tribes, you made a point of playing off one tribe against another in order to rule them all. Clearly he left no opportunities of this kind unexploited.

Up to the attack on St Albans, Boudica had had things all her own way, taken the initiative, and made good use of it. After St Albans, her luck ran out and she was no longer able to influence events. Whatever move she made now would be in the nature of a desperate gamble. For Suetonius, the position was hardly less critical. He had won Wales only to lose East Anglia. For the moment, he was cut off from Roman Gaul, as he could not know to what extent there was support for Boudica in Kent, the nearest part of Britain to the continent. He had sacrificed London and St Albans in order to find a battle site to his advantage, so that he might save the whole province. He and 10,000 of his troops stood between the holding together of the Roman Empire and the breakaway of its north-western edge. If Boudica were to win back Britain for the Celts, what was to stop the revolt spreading to Gaul and succeeding there?

The issue could not be left in doubt any longer. Suetonius decided that he must lure Boudica into battle. As soon as he joined up with Legio XIV and Legio XX, probably at High

Cross, or perhaps at Wall, he sent out scouts to survey the area and find a number of possible battle sites. Tacitus and Dio Cassius described the battle but, maddeningly for us in the present century, did not say or hint at where it took place. Probably they assumed their readers would know, or at least have heard of the great battle which may have had a name familiar to Romans. Archaeologists have been able to help to some extent. There were forts at Wall and at Mancetter (Manduessedum) both along Watling Street. There may have been one at High Cross (there was certainly one there later). The three locations are in a straight line north-westwards, High Cross about 10 miles south-east of Mancetter and Wall about 15 miles north-west of Mancetter. If there was no fort then at High Cross, Suetonius could have constructed a temporary camp for his men, a standard Roman practice on campaign. Any one of the three military sites could have been the supporting base for the army when it finally brought Boudica to battle. A convincing case for a battlefield site has been made by Dr Graham Webster, in his study of Boudica.*

Tacitus wrote that Suetonius chose a position in a defile, that is, a narrow valley of some length, with a wood behind him.† Webster considered the terrain between Wall and Mancetter, along and closely on either side of Watling Street, particularly stretches of rising ground. At Mancetter, near Atherstone, a ridge of quartzite rock, the object of extensive quarrying over the past two centuries, runs north-westwards along the south side of the small river Anker meeting Watling Street. Although the quarrying has clearly altered the shape of the ridge, Dr. Webster visualizes several possible defiles there that satisfy Tacitus's brief description, and opts for one which overlooks the site of the Roman fort beside the Anker at Mancetter, first identified in 1955-56 and confirmed in later, more detailed excavation. Taking this to be the site — which we may safely do until someone comes up with a better one‡, the forces of Suetonius could have been drawn up on the northern slopes of the ridge, with the protecting woods behind, looking down upon the plain below through which Watling Street runs and where to the left it crosses the Anker. And in the plain Boudica's host could have been massed.

When Suetonius finally determined his positions in front of

*Boudica, Graham Webster, Batsford, 1978, pp. 96-98 and 111-112.

†Tacitus, Annals, xiv. 34, (p. 319).

‡Though we cannot entirely discount the more conventional view that the battle took place near High Cross, where similar terrain is found.

the wood, he assembled and drew up his troops in an arc. In the centre were three formations of legionaries, one behind the other. On either side were two detachments of auxiliaries — foot-soldiers in this case — and on the wings were the cavalry. He had probably mustered about 12,000 troops, a small complement compared with the six-figure British force milling about in the open plain.

Boudica, meanwhile, had discovered from advance scouts where Suetonius was planning to draw up, and what the scouts told her encouraged her to make ready her host and to engage without delay. The host was assembling several hundred yards down the slope in the plain, jostling and pushing and running about, with little pretence to forming tidy ranks or squadrons. Britons on horseback mingled with men and women warriors on foot. There were hundreds of chariots being driven about all the available space by drivers anxious to whip up enthusiasm among the foot-soldiers. Behind the great mass of British fighting men and women, other women and children were hustling waggons and carts into one or two long lines, end-to-end across the lower part of the battlefield, effectively sealing off any possible escape from the field on the British side. Tacitus says the wives and children had come to watch the battle, confident that the warriors, in their enormous numerical superiority, of at least ten to one, would win the day. No one on the British side seems to have considered the bad position of their forces. No one grasped that when the signal for attack came they would be charging uphill and for quite a distance.

Boudica, meanwhile, drove round the field in her chariot, probably with her two daughters in front, gripping the rails of the wickerwork sides. Here and there went the queen, a tall and magnificent figure in full battle array, this time perhaps wearing a dyed tunic and trousers with a striped cloak fastened round her neck by a splendidly ornate silver brooch and perhaps the twisted golden necklace again. Possibly, she had sewn on to the belt round her waist one or two little bells, which would have rung out every time the chariot wheels bounced against a molehill or slipped momentarily into a rut in the ground, so that her people, wherever she went, would know she was with them, encouraging them forward.

Tacitus reports a heroic speech she made to her huge army on that crucial day of battle. He sums it up in a few lines, some of which we may give in translation:

"We British are used to women commanders in war. I am fighting as an ordinary person for my lost freedom, my bruised body and my outraged daughters. The gods will give us the vengeance we deserve! The Roman division that dared to fight is annihilated.* The others cower in their camps. They will never face even the din and roar of all our thousands, much less the shock of our onslaught. Look and see how many of you are fighting—and what you are fighting for—and why! Then you will win this battle, or perish."†

Suetonius is also reported to have made a defiant but much less flowery speech to his relatively small army, and Tacitus's rendering is probably the kind of thing he would have said. Tacitus had soldier relatives and he knew how Roman generals addressed their men before battle.

"Don't pay any attention to the noises of these savages. They are unwarlike and ill armed: when they see the weapons and valour of troops who have beaten them so often they're going to crack. Keep together: throw your javelins when I tell you; then strike with your swords and hit them with the bosses of your shields; mow them down. Don't give a thought to booty. Win the victory, and you'll get the lot."‡

Among the British there was a growing impatience to get on with the fighting. Some of the more unruly of the warriors started to scream and shout, roaring out their fearsome battle songs, so loudly that when Boudica ordered the signal to be sounded by the heralds with their oxhorns, the noisier chiefs and their followers did not hear. The British masses began to move forwards, not in orderly ranks but in a mob-like rush, like a mass of angry demonstrators against the government in a modern Middle Eastern state or a crowd of football team supporters who have lost their self-control at a match and broken out on to the field. The Romans remained still and quiet, inwardly amused, no doubt, at the antics of these strange warriors who brought their families with them on to the battlefield.

The British accelerated in a run, but before long they found it hard going up the slope. Their pace slowed into a laboured

*Petillius Cerealis's vexillation from Legio IX (see p. 55).

†*Annals*, xiv. 35, (p. 320).

‡*Annals*, xiv. 36, (p. 320), paraphrased.

walk for many, while others found it less tiring, giving the front lines an overall straggling look. The shouting and singing continued the while, and the din of the warriors mingled with the clatter of the armaments they carried and the many trumpets that were constantly being blown by over-excited heralds and perhaps others, so that "all the country round had got a voice and caught up the cry". It must have been terrifying for the Romans, but still they did not flinch nor move.

Where were the chariots? Boudica did not at first send them up to the front. She thought there were quite enough troops walking and riding to overwhelm the Roman force squeezed — as it appeared to her — into the clearing between the two "prongs" of woodland near the top of the hill. The chariots could stay in reserve, she thought. Their time would come, as it so often did in battles in which the Celts fielded armies.

The British host edged closer to the defile, but the Romans waited until they judged that the enemy front lines were within javelin's throw. Then, Suetonius gave the order for javelins to be hurled, and almost in unison the legionaries lunged forward, loosing a concerted and deadly hail of sharp iron weaponry into the seething mass lurching breathlessly up the slope and into the defile. The British advance was momentarily checked: at that moment the legionaries, sheltered behind their protective shields, pulled out their swords and charged downhill, well disciplined and in wedge-shaped formations. Backed up by the auxiliary infantry behind and at their sides, they cut a series of huge holes in the dense throng of the warriors. Up came the swords jabbing at close quarters like daggers, with terrifyingly murderous effect. For every Roman who might be felled by a Celt wielding a slashing long sword about his head, half a dozen Britons would with certainty be despatched by short, sharp jabs in an appropriate part of the body by one Roman legionary. And the Britons hated these Roman sword tactics. They squirmed and turned in their tracks to avoid them, and got into each other's way, adding to the confusion that was gathering momentum everywhere in the British ranks.

Then the Roman cavalry were ordered to charge. Each mounted soldier raised his lance, extended it forward, and at the signal, jabbed his heels into the flanks of the brave animals who so often carried their riders through every conceivable ordeal in warfare, and catapulted forwards. In steady formation, the horsemen moved down the hill, diagonally, one squadron to the left and the other to the right, at the outer ends of the Roman lines, and charged at the groups of Britons trying to get out of the general shambles. In their hundreds the Britons were cut down where they stood, or they were pursued and killed as they attempted to leave the battlefield.

Some time during the day, Boudica, not one to stand in safety behind the rear lines, plunged into the fray, urging her warriors on to great deeds of valour, performing them herself, no doubt, as well. Probably, when she saw the front lines crumpling under the onslaught of the Roman wedge formations, she ordered the charioteers to come to the edge of the mêlée. The warriors in the chariots then jumped down and rushed in, for they were especially brave and skilled people, "knocking the Romans helter-skelter", but because they were not armoured with breast plates they succumbed to volleys of arrows from Roman archers and many were put out of action. Other drivers would leap into the empty vehicles and drive them out of the battle area and then turn and charge back in again, only to be brought down by a shower of arrows. It was carnage on a large scale. Despite their enormous numerical superiority, Boudica's forces were not equal to the solid, disciplined, precision-functioning Roman military machine.

It was the Roman cavalry that broke the remainder of the organized units of the British army, and as it did, the whole mass of the host that was still fighting began to break up and run. It must have taken hours for so many people to try to get out of the plain that day, chased by Roman infantrymen and cavalrymen, now certain of victory and spurred on by the knowledge that they had probably dealt the death blow to the revolt and thus saved the province. It was late in the day, Dio Cassius says, when the Romans finally prevailed. The last phase was the wholesale slaughter of thousands of Boudica's host who, in their flight from the field, found their outlets blocked by the string of waggons and carts on which their women and children had for much of the day been standing and cheering, but who were now wailing and screaming. Hemmed in on all sides, the Britons were cut down where they stood. Nor were the women spared. And Tacitus adds that even some of the animals were pierced with weapons and piled upon the heaps of the dead. Suetonius and his army had turned a situation of extreme danger into a remarkable military triumph. He had restored the authority of Rome and shown those in Britain who had not chosen to join the revolt that they had made the right judgment.

Ancient historians often claimed very large numbers of people to be involved in great battles, which seem to us to be a little exaggerated. Tacitus quoted a report that almost 80,000 Britons were killed at the battle, which must mean that Boudica's army had exceeded 100,000 at the beginning. Dio Cassius said that Boudica rode at the head of an army of 230,000.* If we accept the 80,000 dead, it is still an enormous number of people to be killed in a day in one small area, equalled in our time by the number of people who died in the first hour or two after the explosion of the atomic bomb on the Japanese city of Hiroshima, in August 1945. But frightful though that was, it represented but a fraction of the total population of Japan. Boudica's 80,000 dead was probably more than one tenth of the Celtic population of all Britain at the time.

At the other end of the scale, we may be surprised to learn from Tacitus that only 400 Romans died, less than one per cent of the strength of the Roman army in Britain. If he is right, Suetonius's victory for Rome was indeed "glorious and comparable with bygone triumphs" (Tacitus). His men could certainly be proud of acquitting themselves in the best traditions of the greatest army in the world. When he heard the news, Poenius Postumus, the camp prefect in charge of Legio II at Exeter, committed suicide by falling on his sword. He had cheated his men of taking part in this splendid page of Roman military history by refusing to obey Suetonius's orders to join him on Watling Street before the abandonment of London.

The two figures of the battle—indeed of the whole revolt—who interest us most are Boudica and Suetonius. The revolt had been a test of their respective skills, their powers of leadership and their ability to handle situations favourable and unfavourable. And Boudica had lost. She had failed to take Britain out of the Roman Empire, an honourable and praiseworthy ambition, for all people must be free to choose their own leaders and their own form of government. Now, there had to be a reckoning. The British could not expect that no vengeance should be exacted on them. Boudica knew very well she would receive no mercy at all. Not for her the journey to Rome, the pardon and the pensioning off that Caratacus

*Dio, lxii. 8, (p. 97).

enjoyed. Suetonius would not be able to overlook the butcheries by her followers in Colchester, London and St Albans. She fled from the battlefield, probably back to her lands in Norfolk. But then, what?

Boudica vitam veneno finivit: Boudica put an end to her life with poison. With this short sentence Tacitus abruptly makes his last reference to the great queen.* He then devotes three paragraphs to the next few months in the career of Suetonius. He is no longer interested in the woman who had for a few months produced the greatest threat to the Roman Empire since the destruction of three legions by the German chief, Arminius, in the Teutoberger Forest in 9 A.D. Dio Cassius, writing over a century after the events, says that Boudica got away from the Midlands and then fell sick and died. † The Britons mourned her deeply and gave her a costly burial. These are the only two comments that are of any use in reconstructing the circumstances of her end. And it is likely that the answer lies somewhere between the two. After his victory, Suetonius spent much of the weeks that followed pursuing groups of escaping Britons and punishing sternly those who continued to offer resistance. Possibly some were encouraged by Boudica once she had got back to her kingdom. It was a last hopeless gesture of defiance, and she must soon have realized it was a waste of time. Perhaps she may have heard that a detachment of Roman cavalry was scouring the Norfolk countryside looking for her. The Roman reputation for thoroughness would have convinced her that sooner or later they would catch up. There was really nothing left but to end it all, and without any fuss she took poison, some fatal drops, maybe, in a last cup of British beer which she drank toasting the gods who had watched over her in her gallant stand for Celtic freedom.

The Celts were accustomed to giving their heroes splendid funerals, and women warriors were no less honoured than men. If Dio Cassius is right, Boudica's funeral could have been as magnificent as any. She could have been laid on her back along the platform of her chariot, her weapons placed beside her, with her helmet and shield and, perhaps, the royal ornaments, including the famous twisted golden necklace — and all the treasure, too. Did her attendants put down beside

Annals, xiv. 37, (p. 321).

†Dio, lxii. 12, (p. 105).

her body some jars of beer and some plates of food for a feast they expected her to have in her next life? Such were the kind of objects found in many Celtic warriors' tombs in Europe. But if this is how she was buried, the whereabouts of the burial site remains a mystery. All that survives are her name and the legends that it has inspired.

EPILOGUE

Boudica's rebellion may have cost the British people more than a tenth of their population killed. Many thousands more had been wounded, some so badly that they were never able to work again, or to enjoy a full life. The timing of the revolt, favourable to them in the short term because Suetonius was more than 200 miles away in Wales, was to cost them dear in the longer term. Farming in the East came to a standstill during the secret preparations for rebellion: their fields were left unsown. Once the revolt was on, food became more and more difficult to get and the great host had to dip into precious reserves. The rebels failed to capture the Roman stocks that they had reckoned on. And when the revolt was over, there were practically no crops to harvest. Tacitus speaks of a famine: there must have been widespread shortages and many survivors will have been close to starvation.

That was not all. Suetonius was determined to stamp out all traces of rebellion. Extra troops were transferred from Europe to Britain and these included 1,000 fresh cavalry. Hostile or wavering tribes were laid waste with fire and sword, says Tacitus.* The kingdom of the Iceni was probably devastated worst of all as it had been the source of the revolt. Suetonius was infected by the same spirit of revenge as Boudica, and his troops obviously shared his feelings.

The government at Rome, meanwhile, sent a replacement for Catus Decianus, the procurator, whose rapacity had set off the revolt. He was Gaius Julius Alpinus Classicianus, who was not a Roman by birth but a provincial from Upper Gaul, who had earned Roman citizenship about 20 years earlier. Classicianus was not brought up in the same traditions as Suetonius, though he shared the latter's honesty and courage. He did not have the urge for vengeance and he soon saw that the discontented parts of Britain would be more easily pacified by constructive rather than destructive policies. Almost from the beginning of his term, he was at odds with Suetonius because he could not get the old soldier to stay his hand, and within weeks he wrote to the emperor that the troubles in Britain would continue as long as Suetonius remained governor. Nero responded by sending to Britain one of his trusted imperial secretaries, the ex-slave Polyclitus, to examine the state of the province and make a report. Polyclitus arrived in October 61, and after a swift but thorough investigation, he recommended conciliation. The British would, in his view, cooperate with a new governor. And when Suetonius showed that he would not change his policy, he was recalled, though the actual reason for his recall was that he had lost some ships during his pursuit of the rebels. The emperor appointed a new governor, Publius Petronius Turpilianus, who may not have arrived in Britain until early 62. He introduced the milder approach that Polyclitus had suggested, and this was to be the beginning of a period of peace and development. There would be lapses, revolts would be suppressed, tribes would be punished, but there would never again be anything like the rebellion of Boudica and all that it brought to Britain. The Celts began to accept a degree of Romanization and perhaps even to enjoy it. The Romans on their part discovered that their way of life was likely to be more attractive to subject peoples if it was introduced with more caution and more humanity.

General Bibliography

THERE is a vast and growing literature on Iron Age and Roman Britain. Below is a selection of works that will enable the reader to probe the subject in greater depth.

Celtic History
Celtic Britain. Nora Chadwick, Thames & Hudson, 1964.
The Celts. Nora Chadwick, Pelican Books, 1977 (reprint).
The Celts. T. G. E. Powell, Thames & Hudson, 1958 (1967 reprint).
Everyday Life of the Pagan Celts. Anne Ross, Batsford, 1970.
The Personality of Britain. Sir Cyril Fox, National Museum of Wales, 1944.

Romano British History
The Archaeology of Roman Britain. R. G. Collingwood and I. A. Richmond, Methuen, 1969.
Boudica. Graham Webster, Batsford, 1978.
Britain and Julius Caesar. C. F. C. Hawkes, British Academy, 1978.
Britannia. S. S. Frere, Routledge & Kegan Paul, 1978 revised edition.
Camulodunum. Joan & David Clarke, Ginn, 1971.
Camulodunum. C. F. C. Hawkes & M. R. Hull, Society of Antiquaries, 1947.
The Coming of Rome. John Wacher, Routledge & Kegan Paul, 1979.
East Anglia. R. Rainbird Clarke, Thames & Hudson, 1960.
Great Caesar. Plantagenet Somerset Fry, Collins, 1974.
The Great Invasion. Leonard Cottrell, Pan Books, 1961.
Iron Age Farm: the Butser Experiment. Peter J. Reynolds, British Museum Publications, 1979.
Life in Roman Britain. Anthony Birley, Batsford, 5th impression, 1976.
Ordnance Survey Map of Roman Britain. H.M.S.O., 4th edition, 1979.
Roman Britain. I. A. Richmond, Pelican History of England, 1975 (reprint).
Roman Britain. Peter Salway, Oxford University Press, 1981.
Roman Britain. John Wacher, Dent, 1980.
The Roman Conquest of Britain. Graham Webster & Donald Dudley, Pan, 1973.
Roman Fort Defences. Michael Jones, British Archaeological Reports, 21, 1975.
Roman Roads in Britain. Ivan Margary, John Baker, 3rd edition, 1973.
Small Towns of Roman Britain. Warwick Rodwell & Trevor Rowley, British Archaeological Reports, 15, 1975.
Town & Country in Roman Britain. A. L. F. Rivet, Hutchinson University Library, 1975 edition.
The Towns of Roman Britain. John Wacher, Batsford, 1981 (reprint).

Ancient Sources
Caesar, C. Julius. *The Gallic War,* trans. H. J. Edwards, Loeb Classical Library, 1979 reprint.

Caesar, C. Julius. *War Commentaries,* new translation by Rex Warner, Mentor Books, 1960.

Dio Cassius. *Epitome of Books lxi and lxii of his Roman History,* trans. E. Cary, Loeb Classical Library, 1968 reprint.

Suetonius Tranquillus, Gaius. *The Twelve Caesars,* trans. Robert Graves, Penguin Classics, 1958.

Tacitus, P. Cornelius. On Britain and Germany (the *Agricola* and the *Germania*), trans. H. Mattingly, Penguin Classics, 1964 reprint.

Tacitus, P. Cornelius. *Annals,* trans. Michael Grant, Penguin Classics, 1956.

Tacitus, P. Cornelius. *Histories,* trans. Kenneth Wellesley, Penguin Classics, 1964.

Selected articles

The Date of Boudicca's Revolt. Kevin Carroll. *Britannia,* x, 1979, pp. 197-202.

The Coins of the Iceni. D. F. Allen. *Britannia,* i, 1970. pp. 1-33.

Iron Age Coinage in Norfolk. A. K. Gregory. Norfolk Museums Leaflets, 1977.

The Enclosure at Ashill, Norfolk. A. K. Gregory. *Norfolk Archaeology,* 1976.

There are numerous other articles germane to the subject of first century AD Roman Britain in general, and to the Revolt in particular, in the following: *Antiquaries Journal, Antiquity, Archaeologia, Archaeological Journal, Britannia,* Cambridge Antiquarian Society: *Proceedings, Current Archaeology,* East Herts. Archaeological Society: *Proceedings,* Essex Archaeological Society: *Transactions, Journal of Roman Studies, Norfolk Archaeology,* Prehistoric Society: *Proceedings,* Suffolk Institute of Archaeology: *Proceedings.*

Index

J
Jurassic Ridge, 15

K
kings, eleven British k. surrender to Claudius, 34, 64

L
La Tene (Celtic) culture; 12-14
Llyn Cerrig, excavations at: 7, 54
London (Londinium):
  Roman town of: 3,
  Boudica heads for, 57; sacks, 58;
  Suetonius takes small force down to, 58; abandons, 59

M
Maiden Castle, Dorset:
  Celtic hill-fort; 18, 22, 33
Mandubracius, Celtic chief: 18-19

N
Narcissus, secretary to Claudius, quells mutiny on coast of Gaul, 31
Nero, Emperor of Rome, 49
Norwich area, possible site of headquarters of Prasutagus and Boudica: 53

O
oak-trees in Anglesey, 48
ornamental jewellery, Celtic; 14, 25
Ostorius Scapula, Publius;
  second governor of Britain; 36
  ban on weapons, 38; puts down revolt, 37

P
Peddars Way, Roman road: 54, 61
Petillius Cerialis, Q., legion commander at Longthorpe: 3, 55
Plautius, Aulus, Roman general and first governor of Britain: 4, 29;

crosses Thames and sends for Claudius, 32;
deals with mutiny on Gaul coast, 31;
extends military operations in Britain, 33, 35;
retires, 36
Postumus, Poenius, camp prefect at Exeter:
  refuses to send troops from Legio II to meet Suetonius, 63;
  kills himself, 70
Prasutagus, king of the Iceni:
  arrangement with Rome, 5;
  as client-king, 5;
  Boudica's husband, 5, 8, 21;
  death, 8, 42;
  develops agriculture, 41
  grievances build up in reign, 45;
  marriage with Boudica, 26;
  rich, according to Tacitus, 41;
  smooth relations with Rome, 43

R
Richborough (Rutupiae), in Kent:
  Aulus Plautius lands at, 43 AD, 31

S
St Albans (Verulamium):
  Roman town, 3;
  Boudica heads for, 3, 62-63;
  sack of, 63
Scythian tattoo marks, 53fn
Silures, tribe: 36
Snettisham, Norfolk, treasures found at, 40
Spitalfields, remains suggesting scope of fire of London in Boudica's sack, 59
Suetonius Paulinus, Gaius; Roman governor of Britain:
  abandons London, 63;
  arrives in Britain, 45;
  description of, 46;
  destroys druids in Anglesey, 48;
  dispositions in final battle, 65-66

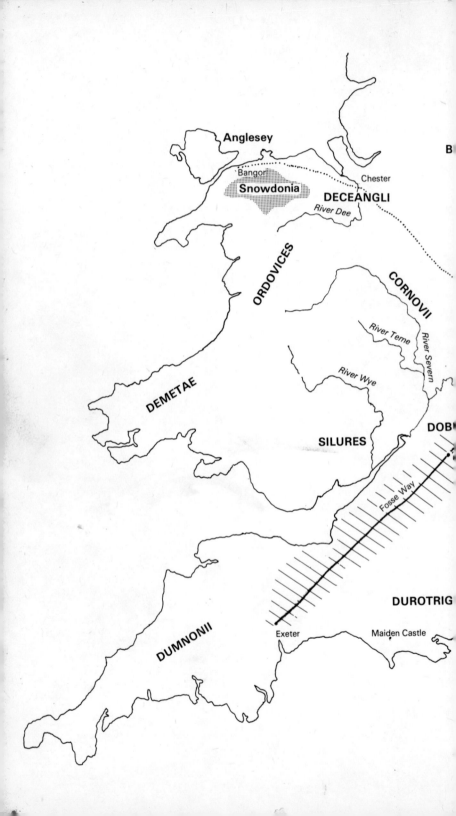